THE OLD TESTAMENT FROM WITHIN

THE
OLD TESTAMENT
FROM WITHIN

BY

GABRIEL HEBERT

of the Society of the Sacred Mission, Kelham
Doctor of Divinity

LONDON
OXFORD UNIVERSITY PRESS
NEW YORK   TORONTO
1962

Oxford University Press, Amen House, London E.C.4

GLASGOW NEW YORK TORONTO MELBOURNE WELLINGTON
BOMBAY CALCUTTA MADRAS KARACHI LAHORE DACCA
CAPE TOWN SALISBURY NAIROBI IBADAN ACCRA
KUALA LUMPUR HONG KONG

PRINTED IN GREAT BRITAIN

PREFATORY NOTE

This book is a completely revised edition of *The Bible from Within*, which was published by the Oxford University Press in 1950. Much of the text of the old book remains, but it is really a new book.

It is offered as a book for the non-theological reader which makes the attempt to show what were the real issues of faith in the various stages of the Old Testament history, and to indicate how these reach their 'fulfilment' in the New Testament. Critical questions are not discussed, since the examination of them would demand an investigation of all the relevant biblical texts and the non-biblical evidence; and there is not space for this here. The reader is referred to larger books for this. Much the best for the ordinary reader is Bernhard Anderson, *The Living World of the Old Testament*; somewhat more advanced is Norman Gottwald, *A Light to the Nations*; and for the scholar, John Bright's *History of Israel*. Wright and Filson's *Westminster Historical Atlas to the Bible* is all but indispensable, both for the maps and for the text; and for the earlier period I may mention my own *When Israel came out of Egypt*, a study of the Exodus, published in 1961.

As in *The Bible from Within*, the text of the English *Revised Version* is used throughout, except in two cases where it was necessary to quote from the *Revised Standard Version*. The R.V. text is convenient because it is a very literal translation.

Kelham, Newark   GABRIEL HEBERT, s.s.m.
March 1962.

CONTENTS

'Understandest thou what thou readest?'

INTRODUCTORY

FEW people are likely to take any serious interest in the Old Testament who do not believe, or hope to be able to believe, that it has a real Word of God to say *to them*. The aim of this book is, if possible, to clear some hindrances out of the way, and to help to make the Old Testament intelligible as a book about real men and women to whom the Word of God came. The words 'from within' in our title mean that we are to look at the Old Testament, not like people who look into the rooms of a house from the outside through the windows, but like those who go inside and get to know the family which lives there; that is to say, to try to see what was the faith by which the people of the Old Testament lived. It is fitting, therefore, that the last two chapters should be devoted to the 'fulfilment' of the Old Testament in Jesus the Messiah, and that elsewhere parallels from Christian experience should be introduced.

Today the anxiety which was widely felt in the not too remote past about the Higher Criticism has largely disappeared; for more and more books are now being written which look at the Bible 'from within'. The critical study of the Bible is, first, *Literary Criticism*. This term is familiar to all who have studied English Literature at school or college; it is the endeavour to see and to evaluate what each writer was seeking to show to the people for whom he wrote, in that place and at that time. Next comes the question what his book meant to later generations who read it and used it. Then there is *Historical Study* proper, which is the endeavour to find out, so far as possible, just what happened, and what the persons in the history were trying to do. This historical study has been a primary aim of biblical study and research for a century and more. Latterly much help has come through the discovery and the deciphering of Egyptian and Mesopotamian records —so that we have the Assyrian king's account of the Exile of

Samaria in 721 B.C. and the Babylonian account of the first deportation from Jerusalem in 598—and from the excavation of very many sites in Palestine, so that it has been proved that Lachish, some 40 miles to the south-west of Jerusalem, was taken by assault about 1220 B.C., and Hazor, far in the north, beyond the Sea of Galilee, in the same period; and there is no doubt that in both places the invaders were the Israelites.

Such historical study is indispensable because the faith of the Bible and of the Church was and is that God *has revealed himself by his action in history*, from the Call of Abraham in the dim past to the beginning of Israel's existence as a nation at the Exodus from Egypt and the Covenant at Sinai, to the Entry into Canaan, to the reign of David when it became a civilized nation under a king, to the Exile when Israel ceased to exist as a political power and yet emerged from the catastrophe with renewed spiritual life, and was taught by the prophets to hope for a future work of Divine deliverance—from all this to Jesus the Messiah and the launching of the Church on its mission to all nations. Such are the historical facts; and the men of the Bible saw in them the 'sacred history' of the continuous action of God in Salvation and Judgment. Hence the Bible story is often described as a Drama in which the LORD is the chief Actor, and the men of many generations play their parts: a Drama of decisive significance for all mankind.

It is therefore of great interest to find that, though the plot of the Drama is all worked out through Israel as God's Chosen People, the first eleven chapters of Genesis make no direct reference to Israel at all, but are concerned with God and his world and Man. These chapters were in fact so arranged by the editors of the first five books of the Bible as to form a sort of *Preface* to the whole, because without such a Preface the story, from Abraham onwards, would not be intelligible. These chapters belong not to history proper, but to prehistory, and give the biblical basis for the understanding of all history.

We have first the Creation-poem: In the beginning God created the heavens and the earth, and Man in his own image, able to make a personal response to him (1. 1–2.3). Then we are told how Man, whose blessedness consisted in making his right response to God, took a wrong turn and chose to refuse that response and go his own way (chs. 2 and 3), so that Man, beginning to learn the arts of civilization, because also corrupt; and now comes the Story of the Flood. It does indeed appear that there was a period of very heavy flooding in Mesopotamia, probably at the end of the last Ice Age; but the biblical Flood-story is really concerned not with an episode in history, but rather with the universal Judgment of God upon Man's sin, and at the same time Salvation through the Judgment—this is the meaning of Noah's Ark. The remaining items of Genesis 1–11 deal with God's ordinance for all the nations of mankind in the Covenant with Noah (9. 1–17), and with the Tower of Babel (11. 1–9), which stands as the type of all the efforts of Man to climb up to heaven, like the Greek Prometheus, and secure happiness for himself—efforts which fail every time.

One more thing must be said before we start. It is that the Bible is concerned *not primarily with Religion but with God* and with faith in him. The word 'religion' has been much used and misused, when highly-placed clerics have talked of a national 'Recall to Religion', when what they really meant was a 'Recall to faith in God'. Today this misuse of the word seems to be becoming less common; and certainly the Bible is not guilty of it. In fact, what we find throughout the Bible, and especially in the Old Testament, is the continual conflict between false religion and a right faith. We can all think of the sin of the Israelites in making the Golden Calf, Exodus 32, or again of the deadly peril to Israel's faith when Jezebel, the princess from Tyre, became queen at Samaria, or of the idolatry of the kings of Judah also later on, who, terrified by the threat of the militarist power of Assyria to Israel's very existence, were tempted to offer sacrifice to any god or gods who might help in their sore need; if one god could not help, perhaps another would.

Against all this stood the rock-like faith of Moses and Elijah and Amos and Isaiah, faith in the LORD who has delivered Israel out of Egypt and who alone was true God, who was the creator of heaven and earth, and who was in control of history; who was himself sending the Assyrians to chastise his faithless people (Isa. 10. 5–15, pp. 67–68 below), and who was the Rock, the sure Foundation (Isa. 28. 16). Again and again in the Bible the steadfast faithfulness of God is contrasted with the spiritual and moral frailty of men.

We start, then, in the first two chapters, with the Preface to the Bible.

CHAPTER I

'*By the Word of the LORD were the heavens made*'

THE CREATION : GENESIS 1

THE CREATION-POEM

THE first chapter of Genesis is a poem, consisting of six cantos, with a rhythm which recurs with variations throughout:

> 'And God said . . .
> And it was so.
> And God made . . .
> And God saw that it was good.
> And there was evening and there was morning,
>   the . . . Day'

till the final canto, when on the seventh Day *God rested,* the work of creation being complete; he kept Sabbath. The rhythm of Israel's own life consisted of six working days and a day of solemn rest:

> 'Verily ye shall keep my sabbaths;
> For it is a sign between me and you throughout your generations,
>   That ye may know that I am the LORD, which sanctify you.'
>
> (Exod. 31. 13)

They are told in the creation-poem that the orderly rhythm of their life was founded on God's own work. Further, Israel too was at last to enter into his rest. Psalm 95 in its last verse reminded them of the peril lest they should fail to enter into that rest through sin, like those Israelites who were disobedient to him in the wilderness, and to whom God swore in his wrath that they should not enter into his rest. There is a commentary on this in the Epistle to the Hebrews (4. 1–13), where it is explained that the 'rest' to which Ps. 95 refers could not there mean the Entry into Canaan under Joshua, v. 8, which those Israelites forfeited by their sin, since the psalm was written long after; its real meaning must be 'the Sabbath-rest which remaineth for the people of God', v. 9, which, as the

Christian readers know, is the messianic Kingdom which Jesus has opened to all believers.

Another point to notice in the creation-poem is that the word *create* occurs only three times, of the creation of the universe, 1. 1, of animal life, 1. 21, and of man, 1. 27, besides its occurrence in the summary at the end, 2. 3. Elsewhere the word 'make' is used: God made the firmament, the sun, moon and stars, the beasts of the earth after their kinds, and man in his own image. It is used also in the Hebrew of 'trees making fruit' with seeds in them (1. 11, 12), where the English versions translate 'yielding' or 'bearing' fruit. Thus God 'creates' things which continue to 'make' themselves by the processes of natural law and reproduction; and when it is said that 'God finished his work', 2. 2, it is not that the created world is finished in the sense in which a machine such as a clock is finished, but rather that it is so created as to contain within itself its powers of growth and renewal.

We notice also that the world which God has created is *good*. There is no suggestion here or elsewhere in the Old Testament of the notion which later became habitual in the Greek world and in other cultures, that matter is evil in itself and fleshly desires are all evil. For the Hebrew, it is man's disloyalty to God that is evil, while 'the whole earth is full of God's glory' (Isa. 6. 3), and 'The heavens declare the glory of God, and the firmament showeth his handi-work' (Ps. 19. 1).

The poem gives a magnificent impression of the *orderliness* of God's creation. The Bible never speaks of 'laws of nature', but the idea is there. It has in fact a double conception, of the Order of Nature and the Order of Righteousness, which God has laid down as his law for man. This latter is not mentioned in the creation-poem, but it becomes explicit later; and the double idea is magnificently expressed in Isa. 45. 18–19:

'Thus saith the LORD that created the heavens,
 He is God,
That formed the earth and made it;
He established it, he created it not a waste,
He formed it to be inhabited:

I am the LORD and there is none else.
I have not spoken in secret, in a place of the land of darkness;
I said not unto the seed of Jacob, Seek ye me, in vain;
I the Lord speak righteousness, I declare things that are right.'

When we thus see the Story of the Creation as a poem, and see that the first eleven chapters of Genesis are a Preface to the Bible, we escape from the danger of setting up a conflict between Faith and Science. Such a conflict arises at once if we think of the Creation as 'the first event in world-history'. The editors of the Authorized Version fell into this trap when they put in the margin opposite Genesis 1. 1 the date '4004 before Christ'. The date was reached by adding up the figures in the biblical genealogies. This was a piece of very naïve literalism, which gave much trouble in the 19th century when sciences such as astronomy and geology were inquiring into the age of the earth and the manner in which the solar system can have come into being, and were learning that the Sun belongs to the Galaxy or 'Milky Way', and that there are innumerable other galaxies in the depths of space. Consequently it seemed that the creation-story in Genesis was simply untrue.

But in fact the creation-poem and the account given by the astronomers lie on different levels. The astronomer is reasoning back from observed facts to try to form some idea of the process by which the sun and the planets and the gaseous nebulae and the galaxies took their present shape. Nuclear physics now show that the structure of matter is atomic, and the vast output of energy in the sun and other stars can be traced back to the formation of molecules of helium out of hydrogen; and somewhere here he comes to a point where, at least at present, he can go no further.

If at this point the theologian yields to the temptation to say, 'Just here we reach the point at which we must affirm a divine act of creation', he is justly rebuked by the scientist for butting in on a rigorous inquiry which depends on observed facts, with an un-proved theological assumption; on his own ground, the scientist is of course right. But in fact he and the theologian are asking different questions and are starting from different points. The theologian is asking, not about the physical process of the formation of suns and planets, but about the meaning and purpose of the whole creation, and about man's place within it; and his thought is thus moving on a wholly different level from that of the scientist, and the facts to which he in turn appeals are facts of a different order. We must now consider what these are; for they are the facts on which the creation-poem in Genesis also depends.

THE BIBLICAL FAITH IN GOD

Where then did the biblical writers learn their doctrine of God?

They believed that God had revealed himself; that is to say, that there had been Action from the Other Side, in which the Divine Being had taken action on their behalf. They had been in Egypt, subject to forced labour, building civil and military works for Pharaoh Rameses II. Word had come to them from Moses that the LORD purposed to deliver them from this oppression and bring them into a country which they were to conquer; and the deliverance had most wonderfully come to pass on a critical night when it had seemed that all was lost, when they had been caught between the pursuing Egyptians and the Red Sea, yet somehow they had crossed the Sea and had found themselves safe on the other side, and free. After this they had gone to Sinai, and the LORD who had delivered them had adopted them as his chosen people and given them his commandments. Then after a period of nomad life in the desert they had gone in and possessed the Land. Such had been the beginning of Israel's existence as a nation; and before this there had been the LORD's call of Abraham.

Hence the typical biblical expression of faith is what Dr. Ernest Wright calls a 'Theology of Recital'; this is the sub-title of his book *God who Acts*. The Israelites delighted to 'rehearse the saving acts of the LORD. We shall see instances of this in chapter III, dating from quite early times; but we may refer here to Psalm 136 (probably composed many centuries later), which has the refrain

'For his mercy (*or* "For his steadfast love") endureth for ever'

after each verse. It begins with praising God, vv. 1–4; then it recites his creation of heaven and earth, sun, moon and stars, vv.

5–9, and immediately after that the deliverance from Egypt in the Exodus, vv. 10–15, and the conquest of the Land, vv. 16–22.

This Theology of Recital is familiar to us Christians. Not only do we accept the Old Testament as part of our Bible; the saving acts of the LORD are continued in the New Testament, and the central part of the Creed consists of a recital of the saving acts of the incarnation and death and resurrection of our Lord, while the same sort of recital reappears in the hymn *Te Deum laudamus*.

The divine work of salvation in the Old Testament and the New needed to be interpreted to men by the Holy Spirit. When the LORD delivered the people out of Egypt, he sent also his servant Moses to interpret what he was doing and call forth their response of faith and obedience; in the great crisis of the Exile, prophets were sent to interpret the LORD's work of Judgment and bring the people through; and in the New Testament, we see our Lord himself interpreting the meaning of his own mission, and after his death and resurrection and the gift of the Holy Spirit the apostles and evangelists did the same, by the light of the Spirit. The revelation of God does not consist in mighty acts which we are left to make sense of as best we can. There is the gift of the Spirit; and now and always, 'he that hath an ear let him hear what the Spirit saith unto the churches.'

FALSE GODS

This being so, it is not surprising that the faith of Israel should have been in continuous conflict with the current beliefs and religious practices of Canaan and Syria; and in fact this conflict lasted throughout the whole period from the Conquest to the Exile. We shall see in later chapters how the Israelites were all too easily led away to the cult of gods who were personifications of natural forces, such as the Canaanite Baals who made the corn grow, and whose favour it seemed to be necessary to secure in order to get a good harvest; hence the prophet Hosea says, in the LORD's Name, 'She did not know that I gave her the corn and the wine and the oil' (Hos. 2. 8). Then, again, there was the notion of a tribal god, who was a personification of the genius of the tribe, so that if a

tribe were overwhelmed in war, it was because its god had been
defeated and overpowered by the stronger gods of its enemies. But
the LORD the God of Israel was different; he had freely chosen
Israel to be his people, and adopted her. Yet nothing was easier
than for Israel to drop away into the common way of thinking, and
to identify his cause with her cause and her success. Israel was set to
learn this lesson the hard way; she could have learnt it from the
prophets, above all the great Isaiah (cf. pp. 66–69 below), but the
pull of nationalist patriotism was very strong, and she never finally
learnt it till she was defeated and overwhelmed, till the City was
destroyed and the temple burnt with fire and the survivors deported
into exile. Then at last she learnt that the LORD was the Lord of
History, who could carry out his purpose with his chosen people
through her political extinction.

So at last she learnt what the teaching of the prophets had never
finally brought home, that 'the LORD, he is God'. They said as
plainly as possible that the ruin of the nation was coming, and their
predictions were most terribly fulfilled. But when it had happened,
all were able to see that the gods whom men made in their own
image were no-gods. Isaiah of Babylon, fifty years after the exile,
ridiculed the gods of the heathen, who could do nothing and
originate nothing:

'Let them bring them forth, and declare unto us what shall happen:
declare ye the former things, what they be, that we may consider them,
and know the latter end of them; or show us things for to come. Declare
the things that are to come after, that we may know that ye are gods; yea,
do good, or do evil, that we may be dismayed and behold it together.
Behold, ye are of nothing, and your work of nought; an abomination is
he that chooseth you' (Isa. 41. 22–4).

In 44. 9–20 there is a highly sarcastic description of a man making
an image of a god, using the waste parts of the wood to make a fire
and cook his dinner, and fashioning the rest into a god, to which he
bows down in worship. In 46. 1–2, at the predicted fall of Babylon,
Bel and Nebo are pictured as loaded up on the back of weary
animals, and carried off. But as for the LORD,

'Even to old age I am He,
And even to hoar hairs will I carry you;
I have made, and I will bear;
Yea, I will carry, and will deliver.
To whom will ye liken me, and make me equal,
And compare me, that we may be like?' (Isa. 46. 4–5).

He was writing these words perhaps a generation before the great creation-poem of Genesis 1 was written down.

We make a great mistake if we think that we, whose civilization has developed so far above the level of those primitive days, need not trouble much about the doctrine of God the creator, as if this were an elementary truth which we can now take for granted. The outward setting has changed, and the names have changed: the fundamental issue remains much the same. Multitudes of people to-day worship false gods. There is the god of Luck: witness the betting and gambling and lotteries and football pools. There is the god or goddess of Lust, drawing a crowd of devotees. There is Mammon, the passion for money-making for the sake of the comforts which it buys, the power over other people's lives which it gives, or the pride of victory in the competition of wits. There is Nationalism, which indeed has altered little from what it was in those old days, except in the vast resources which it has at its disposal both as regards material means of destruction and the power of propaganda to carry the minds of men away in its lust of power.

MODERN HUMANISM

But our belief in God is not only endangered by ways of living and thinking which are generally recognized as deviations. It is directly challenged by the widespread Humanism which can often set itself to uphold the best and noblest ideals, and can even set a high value upon Religion, but firmly refuses to believe in God. Lately I came across some lines of verse about a visit to Canterbury cathedral; the writer was thrilled with its beauty and dignity, and reflected that it was built by men to the glory of God; but he went on to say that such a faith is impossible for us, and that for us

B

Canterbury cathedral is a work of human genius, a monument to the greatness of Man.

In *The Listener* for April 21st, 1960, there was a talk about Humanism by Sir Julian Huxley, not on the Third Programme for the intellectuals, but in 'Woman's Hour' on the Light Programme, in which he said:

'Humanist beliefs are based on human knowledge, especially on the knowledge-explosion of the hundred years since Darwin published *The Origin of Species*, which has revealed to us a wholly new view of the universe and our place in it. We now believe with confidence that the whole of reality is one gigantic process of evolution. This produces novelty and variety, and ever higher types or organization; in a few spots it has produced life, and in a few of these spots of life it has produced mind and consciousness.

This universal process is divisible into three spheres . . . Over most of the universe it is in the lifeless or inorganic phase. On earth (and undoubtedly on other planets of other suns) it is in the organic or biological phase; this works by natural selection, and has produced a large variety of animals and plants, some astonishing organizations (like our own bodies, or an ant-colony), and the emergence of mind. Finally man (and possibly a few other organisms elsewhere) has entered the human, or as we may call it, the psychological stage, which is based on the accumulation of knowledge and the organization of experience.'

We Christians share this evolutionary outlook; we know that we look out on an immeasurably vast universe; can we still think that Man is as important in the whole scheme of things as the Christian faith in God as Creator and Redeemer proclaims that he is? We can reflect that the psalmist also asked this question:

'When I consider thy heavens, the work of thy fingers,
The moon and the stars, which thou hast ordained,
What is man, that thou art mindful of him,
Or the son of man, that thou visitest him?' (Ps. 8. 3–4.)

We admire the immensity and spendour of the Sun; and we now know that the splendour of Sirius or Capella, which are many times larger than the Sun, must be far greater. Yet we reflect also that the immensity of the Sun and Sirius and Capella is only a material immensity; and we cannot think that in these mighty suns there is any response to our admiration of them, or any gratitude for it. Such response is a spiritual quality, which could only exist in a Mind which called those suns into existence. And this is the answer which the psalmist makes to his own question, 'What is man?' He says

> 'Thou has made him but little lower than God,
> And crownest him with glory and honour;
> Thou makest him to have dominion over the works of thy hands.'
> (Ps. 8. 5–8.)

Thus the glory of God is manifested, not only in the starry heavens, but also in man whom he has made in his own image; and so he concludes

> 'O LORD, our Lord,
> How excellent is thy Name in all the earth' (v. 9).

Humanists do not wish to be materialists. Yet there is a tendency towards materialism in the scientific outlook, because the quest of science is to find law and order in Nature, and thus to see Nature as a vast mechanism in process of evolution. Dogmatic materialism affirms that it is matter that is essentially real, and that Life and Mind have evolved or emerged out of Matter as a sort of bye-product or *epiphenomenon*. There is therefore no reality in human ideals and hopes and visions and theories, what is real is certain movements in the grey matter of human brains; for living things all die when their time comes, and man dies also, and then, in another psalmist's words, 'all his thoughts perish' (Ps. 146. 4). But the odd thing here is, that the materialistic theory itself is a creation of man's mind, and if all human thoughts and theories are evanescent and ultimately unreal, it follows that the theory of materialism also is unreal—and not true.

If materialism were true, there would be no answer to give to the question 'What is Man?' except to say in the words of Hobbes, that his life is 'nasty, brutish and short'. And has the Humanist, who does not want to be a materialist, but leaves God out of the picture and seeks to glorify Man, any other answer to the question? Can he really hold that Man is a *person*, until he becomes a Christian Humanist?—till he learns to say with the author of Psalm 146, not only that Man must die and his thoughts perish, but as in the next verse,

> 'Blessed is he that hath the God of Jacob for his help,
> And whose hope is in the LORD his God.' (Ps. 146. 5.)

If we deny God and his glory, is there any foundation left on which to erect a doctrine of the glory of Man? The teaching of the whole Bible is that the life of Man falls into its right place only when that place is acknowledged to be *a subordinate place*, and that it is of God's glory, not of Man's, that heaven and earth are full.

If this is so, what follows from it? It follows that the amazing vista which Science has opened up for us of the immensity of the starry heavens does not in any way prove that it is impossible for man to believe in God and call him Father. Actually it gives us a far wider view than was possible in pre-scientific days of the Infinity of God. Yet after all, we have all that we need in the words spoken in the LORD's Name by Isaiah of Babylon—

> 'My thoughts are not your thoughts,
> Neither are your ways my ways, saith the LORD.
> For as the heavens are higher than the earth,
> So are my ways higher than your ways,
> And my thoughts than your thoughts.' (Isa. 55. 8–9.)

MAN IN GOD'S IMAGE

What does it mean, that Man is made in God's image? Something like this: that while his thoughts are not as God's thoughts, and God has planned his universe and has his purpose for it and for man within it, man in his subordinate place can think what that purpose is, and understand it in part, along one line by patient scientific inquiry, or along another line by thinking theologically. Such theological thinking is not for learned people only; the ordinary Christian has a sense of his vocation, that is, of God's purpose for him. God creates a universe which is inconceivably vast, and yet so inconceivably minute that (as we are told) there are seventy thousand million million million atoms in an ounce of uranium; but man too can create, out of materials provided for him in God's universe, his locomotives and ocean liners; his scientific knowledge; the *Midsummer Night's Dream*, Beethoven's Ninth Symphony, Turner's paintings, Epstein's sculptures, Salisbury cathedral; while each housewife fashions and creates her own home, impressing on it something of her personality, so that each home in a street is different from every other. Man's life is lived within the natural order; but he is not a mere cog in a machine, but is able to stand outside it, survey it, make judgements upon it.

He has a sense of Truth: that there is a truth which can be reached by disinterested and unprejudiced research, in which the personal desires of the investigator and all wishful thinking are as far as possible eliminated, and that this apprehension of truth, though always limited and imperfect, is nevertheless real. Such is the way of scientific research.

He has a sense of a Right and Wrong which are independent of the desires and ambitions of men. The fact that a practice or habit exists is no proof that it is good; opium-smoking is an instance. Might is no criterion of Right. There is a good worth living for, and therefore also worth dying for.

He is subject to Law, not merely to the 'positive law' of state legislation, but to the higher 'natural law' by which the law of the state is to be judged. In civilized nations conscientious objectors are allowed the freedom that they demand, even by judges who regard them as self-opiniated and stupid people. In civilized nations it is a fundamental principle that the Judiciary must be separate from the Executive: in other words, that those who preside in the law-courts shall not be responsible to the Government in power. The State must not be judge in its own case.

He believes that there is a common humanity which possesses rights. The true principle of Democracy is that the citizens are not mere members of a hive, but possess a certain authority in relation to the affairs of the hive. They are men, and have a right to sit in judgement on the actions of the State, and criticize the laws which they obey.

These are permanent principles on which our civilization has stood. But they depend on a doctrine of the nature of man which is ultimately a theological doctrine; for this doctrine of man asserts that he is something more than an animal, something more than a bundle of psychological impulses, something more than a mere unit in a social organism. He belongs to the created order, he is moulded by heredity and environment; but he is also a person. The fact that he is a person means that he belongs also to an eternal order, has a sense of truth and a sense of right, and can believe in God. When therefore the creation-story in Gen. 1 says that man is made in God's image, it is proclaiming man's freedom and man's character as a responsible person, able to create in his own subordinate way.

Recent history has made it clear that when belief in God is lost sight of, each of these points that we have stated is liable to be lost too. Men are treated as subjects for 'conditioning' or propaganda; right comes to be identified with the claims of the totalitarian State; the State insists on being judge in its own cause; the rights of common humanity are set at naught. It is further true that these principles which the totalitarian states deny outright are in peril of being continuously whittled away in the so-called Democracies.

CREATION AND REDEMPTION

We shall see in the next chapter how God's creation has been marred by Man's sin. Therefore the Bible tells both of Creation and of Redemption; and the redemption is the renewal and restoration of that which God created in the beginning. It is not that by the redemptive work of Jesus Christ man is rescued from entanglement with the created order and with the body—as if man were thereby raised from preoccupation with the ordinary concerns of life into some region of Higher Thought where he can be initiated into a theosophical secret lore. It is that the Son of God in his Incarnation became true man, growing up in a family, working in a carpenter's shop, and at last facing death as we all must and so winning the victory for man. St. John in his Epistle sees the key-point of the Christian faith in 'Jesus Christ come in the flesh'; every person speaking with authority and claiming inspiration ('every spirit') who confesses this is of God, and he who denies this is utterly and fatally wrong (1 John 4. 1–3).

The world which God has redeemed is the world which he created. This is why St. John's gospel begins with the same words as the Book of Genesis: 'In the beginning God created the heavens and the earth' (Gen. 1. 1) and 'In the beginning was the Word . . . by whom all things were made. . . . And the Word was made flesh and dwelt among us . . .' (John 1. 1, 3, 14).

CHAPTER II

'As in Adam all die . . .'

THE GARDEN OF EDEN: GENESIS 2–3

THE story of Adam and Eve is by a different writer, and it was written before the Exile; it is clear that when we come to Gen. 2. 5 we pass to a different style. But those who compiled our book of Genesis placed this account of Man's life in the world, first as God meant it to be, then as it actually is, next after the great poem of the creation. The writer is telling us, in the form of a tale, about Man's life in general; this is clear from the fact that the Hebrew word *'adam* means simply 'man', and so is not a proper name. The story of Adam and Eve is a common subject for mockery; but the mockery is out of place, for the writer has exceedingly profound things to say to us about ourselves, as we shall seek to show. He has chosen the form of a Tale as the most suitable means for expressing his meaning; and so indeed it is.

Was there a Fall of Man? Was there a first sin? The dogmatic theologian will wish to say that there was. But he is compelled to add that this story in Gen. 2 and 3 cannot possibly be a historical record of the event; no historian could assert that it has any claim to be an authentic memory, handed down in a historical tradition. It comes to us as a Tale, embodying some vital truths about human nature.

MAN'S ORIGINAL AND PROPER CONDITION

First the writer shows us Man's right and proper condition, as God intended him to be. Let us begin with 2. 15: 'The Lord God took the Man, and put him into the Garden of Eden, to dress it and to keep it.' We are in the world 'to dress it and to keep it': to till the soil, build houses, make roads and harbours, get the coal, build up a civilization. 2. 16: 'of every tree in the garden thou mayest freely eat': we have a free hand, we are to use our discretion, and do as we will. But (2. 18) there are things that we must not do: 'the tree of the knowledge of good and evil, thou shalt not eat of it, for in the day that thou eatest thereof thou shalt surely die'. We must say more of the penalty of death later, and of the meaning of 'knowledge of good and evil'; indeed, on the correct understanding of these two points the whole interpretation of the story of the Fall depends. But, leaving these for the moment, we have this clear point: that we are free to do as we will in God's world, but we are subject to his law. While Man so lives, obedient to his will, and receiving everything from him as his gift, and giving him thanks for everything, all is well.

2. 18: 'It is not good that the Man should be alone'; he needs a help suited to him, a companion for life. Such companionship the animals cannot provide. 2. 19, 20: the animals are with the Man in the world, and the LORD God shows them to him, and he gives them names. This we have done. But, 2. 20, the animals cannot provide the companionship he needs; 'for Man there was not found a help meet for him'. Then 2. 21–2: the LORD God brings the Woman to the Man. When he sees the Woman, the Man bursts into the first primal love-song, the type of all his love-songs ever since: '*This* is now bone of my bones, and flesh of my flesh: *this* shall be called Woman ['*Ishshah*], for *this* was taken out of Man ['*Ish*].' The Man has the 'help meet for him'; he recognizes the Woman as the missing half of himself; he was made for her, and she for him. 2. 24: the writer digresses to point out that here is the primal ordinance of Marriage.

We have seen God's ordinance for Man, the pattern of human life, as it was meant to be, lived in God's world and in dependence upon him. Now we come to Man's actual condition, and hear the story of the Fall.

THE FALL OF MAN AND HIS PRESENT CONDITION

3. 1: 'The Serpent' is not explained. No doubt we shall identify it with Satan; but this is not done in the Tale, where nothing is said of the origin of the power of evil to beguile and deceive, and the fact of beguilement and temptation is just accepted. 3. 2–3: the Serpent

asks the Woman about the condition of their life, and she tells it. Then it says, 3. 4, 'Ye shall not surely die, for God doth know that in the day ye eat thereof, your eyes shall be opened, and ye shall be as God, knowing good and evil.' What does this mean?

The Serpent tells them that they will not die, if they break God's law; and seemingly this is quite true, for according to the course of events in the Tale, they do not immediately die, but go on living for a long time, and sons are born to them. But assuredly the writer did not mean that the penalty of death was an idle threat, or a piece of bluff, on God's part. We had best look at the actual consequences of their act; they are as follows:

3. 7: they become aware that they are naked, and are ashamed of it. 3. 8: they run away from God; they 'hid themselves from the presence of the LORD among the trees of the garden'; and they had never done this before. 3. 12: when they are called to account for their action, the Man forgets all that he had said about the Woman being 'bone of his bone and flesh of his flesh'; he speaks of her as 'the Woman whom thou gavest to be with me,' another individual with whom he must get along somehow. There is indeed a change in him; and we read as we go on how (3. 16) to the Woman child-birth is to be hard and painful and (3. 17) to the Man labour becomes drudgery. And then (3. 23) the Man and the Woman have to be turned out of the garden where they have lived in God's presence.

Does not this throw light on the meaning which the writer intends to give to *the penalty of death?* It has often been assumed that 'death' means the death of the body, and those who have taken the story of the Fall as 'literally true' have believed that man before the Fall was immortal; this, however, is impossible for us to take seriously, since we know that Man has evolved from lower forms of life, and death is universal in the animal creation. But the writer cannot have meant this, since it is inconsistent with the course of his own tale. The Serpent indeed so interprets the penalty of death; but the Serpent's mind is bounded by its narrowly materialistic outlook. Actually in the story that which happens to Man is something much worse than bodily death. That which dies in him is his manhood. If we look on further in the Bible we find this point developed by St. Paul in Rom. 8. 6–7: 'The mind of the flesh *is* death,' for 'the mind of the flesh *is* enmity against God'.

But now, what is their sin? Is it the mere transgression of an arbitrary command, the doing of something not wrong in itself, and only wrong because it has been forbidden? We might compare the rule forbidding the Jews to eat pork, which is in itself good food. But if we have already seen reason to think that this writer has very wise things to say, we ought to suspect that the meaning of the prohibition goes deeper than that. Let us inquire, then, into the meaning of *knowing good and evil*. Does it mean 'knowing the difference between right and wrong', by doing evil and so knowing what evil is? That is commonly assumed to be the meaning.

But quite apart from the phrase in 3. 4: 'Ye shall be as God, knowing good and evil,' which on this interpretation would imply that God must do wrong in order to know what it is, this assumption is not consistent with the meaning of 'knowing good and evil' in the other places where it occurs in the Old Testament. There the meaning is consistently the same. 'Knowledge of good and evil' is the attainment of *savoir faire*, sagacity, and capacity to deal with affairs, to which a child attains as it grows up. Infants are without it (Deut. 1. 39; Isa. 7. 15–16); an old man of eighty says in 2 Sam. 19. 35 that he is, as we should put it, 'in his second childhood'. In Gen. 24. 50 a similar phrase comes, with the meaning that the matter in hand has been settled by divine guidance, and cannot be argued on grounds of worldly prudence. Most clearly of all, when young King Solomon is asked by God in a dream what he will have (1 Kings 3. 9), he asks that he may have an understanding heart to judge the people, and 'discern between good and evil', and the gift is granted. What Solomon received is not conscientiousness, but sagacity, prudence, astuteness; this is illustrated by his cleverness in dealing with the problem of the two women with one living baby (1 Kings 3. 16–28).

What then is the sin? To desire to be as God, knowing good and evil, to grow up to the stature of manhood in their own way, worshipping the self instead of God, to develop their intelligence and resourcefulness and capacity to deal with affairs, regardless of God.

The Serpent had suggested (3. 5) that God was keeping something back from them: well then, let them take the course of their lives into their own hands, and (instead of being content to receive from him in dependence and thankfulness the development of their own powers) insist on grabbing at the good things of life, in order to possess them for themselves and grow up in their own way and not his.

Something like this is surely what the writer intends us to understand. And such is human life as we know it and as he knew it too. When we have read a little further in the Book of Genesis we come to the words 'The earth was corrupt before God, and the earth was filled with violence . . . for all flesh had corrupted his way upon the earth' (6. 11–12). Such is the world as we know it, a dark and sinful world.

And yet God has not left Himself without witness, nor is Man totally depraved. As F. D. Maurice says: 'Brutal violence, men corrupting their ways upon the earth—this is just what we hear of everywhere. Scripture had nothing new to tell us about this. But it had a work of its own. It had to teach us how these facts are compatible with others, apparently quite at variance with them, which ordinary history and our own experience also make known to us. It had to show how this natural corruption could co-exist with a perpetual witness in man's conscience, with a continual strife in his will, against it. And it does this work. It shows us that man, yielding to his nature, resists the law which he was created to obey; that man, given up to himself, yet has God's Spirit striving with him. It shows us how man in himself can have no good thing, and yet how much good he may have, because there is One Who is continually raising him out of himself, imparting to him that which in his own nature he has not' (F. D. Maurice, *Patriarchs and Lawgivers of the Old Testament*, p. 62).

WHAT IS SIN?

Such a view of Sin is certainly characteristic of the Old Testament. It is often said, indeed, that the Old Testament is legalistic, providing us with commandments to keep, where the New Testament gives us principles to follow; that the Old Covenant was one of Law, and the New Covenant one of Grace. It is true indeed that the Judaism of the last three or four centuries before Christ did emphasize law-keeping very strongly; the Pharisees in our Lord's day did so. But that is not true of the Old Testament as a whole; the prophets and the psalmists speak throughout of the personal relation between God and his People, and think of Sin not as the mere breach of an imposed rule, but as unfaithfulness to the personal God.

If we would satisfy ourselves that this really is the general view of Sin in the Old Testament, it is easy to do so by a simple experiment, which is rather like the sinking of a shaft by a mining engineer in order to find whether there is coal underground. Look up the words 'transgress' and 'transgression' as they occur in the Authorized Version, in *Young's Analytical Concordance*, which not only gives the places where the English word occurs, but divides it up according to the several Hebrew or Greek words which it represents. This is a rough test, but a reliable one; and what one finds is this. There are four Hebrew words which are translated 'transgress'; *bagad*, *ma'al*, *'abar*, and *pasha'*. *Bagad* means to 'deal treacherously' with God; the same Hebrew word is used in Judges 9. 23, 'the men of Shechem dealt treacherously with Abimelech', in the course of the rather sordid tale of his attempt to reign over them. The next word, *ma'al*, means an act of wrong doing, a trespass or transgression, as when in Nehemiah 13. 27 some Jews have broken the law of Deuteronomy 7. 3 against marrying foreign wives. The next is *'abar*, which means 'to pass by', and in this connexion to 'go the other way', as when I see someone in the distance whom I do not wish to meet, and walk off in another direction; the word is used in Proverbs 4. 15, of the 'way of wicked men': 'avoid it, pass not by it; turn from it and pass on'. The fourth word translated 'transgress', *pasha'*, means simply 'to rebel', and is used in 2 Kings 1. 1: 'Moab rebelled against Israel after the death of Ahab.'

Here we have four words translated 'transgress', which taken together throw a truly remarkable light on the meaning of Sin. One of the four means 'breaking the rules', and it is interesting to see that this word occurs most often in books dating from the post-exilic period, which was the time of Jewish legalism. The other three express in vivid pictorial ways the meaning of sin against the personal God: to 'deal treacherously', to 'walk the other way', to 'rebel'.

ORIGINAL SIN

This brings us to the further question: What do we mean by Original Sin? This is a large question, and to deal properly with the Biblical teaching about Sin a big book would be needed. But we are commenting on the tale in Gen. 3; and in spite of the fact that the tale necessarily speaks of an act of sin, we ought not to think of a white robe of personal innocence now defiled by an ugly stain. This is not admissible, because the name 'Adam', meaning 'Man', and the name 'Eve', meaning 'Life', show that the Man and the Woman are not being thought of merely as individuals in history. Their sin is the sin of Man; and as the whole pattern of the story shows, that which is being described is the passing of Man from a right relation to God (dependence, thankfulness, obedience) to a wrong relation (independence, rebelliousness, alienation). Man chooses to live without God.

When we so view Man's condition, the metaphor of the stain on the white garment is seen at once to be seriously misleading. It is not that Man has now a stain on his moral character, so that he can no longer have a good opinion of himself and consider himself a meritorious and worthy person. It is that Man himself is wrong, aiming in the wrong direction; and this is the idea denoted by the Greek word for sin, *hamartia*. Here we have the distinction between *hamartia*, Sin (with a capital S), and *hamartēmata*, sins: it is a distinction which the Latin language fails to reproduce, so that we still sing (incorrectly) 'O Lamb of God, that takest away the sins of the world,' when the Greek word in John 1. 29 is the word which means Sin.

Here we have the distinction of actual sin and Original Sin. Actual sin is *acts* committed by such and such a person at such and such a time, by thought, word or deed; Original Sin is the *state* of alienation from God which lies behind. It is a pity if we think of Original Sin legalistically, as if it were a sort of entail, or something which renders us 'prone' to commit actual sins. We do better if we take a lesson from Article IX, which explains Original Sin by referring to the *phronēma sarkos*, or 'mind of the flesh', of which St. Paul speaks in Rom. 8. 6–8: 'The mind of the flesh is death, but the mind of the Spirit is life and peace; because the mind of the flesh is enmity against God, for it is not subject to the law of God, neither indeed can it be; and they that are "in the flesh" cannot please God.'

Here 'flesh' and 'Spirit' are opposed. 'Flesh' cannot in this passage mean 'our physical nature', for in that case the last clause would mean 'no one in this life can please God', and St. Paul proceeds (8. 9) 'But ye are not "in the flesh" but in the Spirit, if so be that the Spirit of God dwelleth in you.' He defines the 'mind of the flesh' as 'enmity against God'. It is the attitude of self-centredness, self-love, the idolatry of the self in place of the worship of God; and as St. Paul had known in his life as a Pharisee, it is entirely compatible with an earnest and self-denying religiousness. 'I thank Thee,' said the Pharisee, 'that I am not as other men are, or even as this Publican.'

The escape from this enmity or alienation (which is Original Sin) cannot be effected by the Self, for then it would have cause to take pride in its own ingenuity in contriving its escape, and manipulating the proper psychological strings to bring about its own conversion. The one way of escape is that the means of escape should be provided by God himself, and be received by Man as a gift: and such is the Christian Gospel. 'Herein is love, not that we loved God, but that he loved us, and sent his Son . . .' (1 John 4. 10). To the soul, convicted of its own sin, and awakened to a response to the mighty love of God which has set it free, the only possible right attitude is humility, namely to see the Self in its right and true proportion to God and the world and other people.

Man's soul, thus redeemed and restored, returns to the right relation to God which is depicted in the second chapter of Genesis: he is in God's garden, and knows that he is there to dress it and keep it. He has indeed tasted of the tree of the knowledge of good and evil and developed his faculties in a multitude of wrong ways, exploiting the resources of the earth and exploiting other men in defiance of the Law of God. For this he has incurred death in manifold ways, has earned the wages of Sin, has known despair and perdition.

Yet at last the Seed of the Woman has bruised the Serpent's head, and has brought Man back to peace with God, back into the garden, there to taste of the Tree of Life, in the midst of the garden. And since the Greek word 'paradise' means 'a garden', it seems probable that it was this that our Lord meant when he said to the dying robber who was crucified with him, 'Today shalt thou be with me in Paradise' (Luke 23. 43).

'As in Adam all die, even so in Christ shall all be made alive.'

CHAPTER III

'Abraham believed God'

FROM ABRAHAM TO JOSEPH: GENESIS 12-50

IF Genesis 1-11 can be called a *Preface* to the Bible, the rest of
the book is an *Introduction* to the *Main Story* of Israel as the LORD's
chosen people, which begins with the Exodus. The Introduction
consists of the stories of Abraham, Isaac, Jacob and Joseph; and it
connects up with the Exodus-story by the fact that at the Call of
Moses, when the LORD reveals himself to him, he says, 'I am the
God of thy fathers, the God of Abraham, the God of Isaac and the
God of Jacob' (Exod. 3. 6). Thus the Call of Abraham, with which
Genesis 12 begins, is the first beginning of the LORD's action towards Israel.

But it is more than this. His promise to Abraham in Gen. 12. 3,
'In thee shall all the families of the earth be blessed', announces a
Salvation for all mankind; and so in Galatians 3. 8 St. Paul sees the
Church's mission to the Gentiles in his own day as the fulfilment
of a divine purpose which had been in operation for sixteen or
more centuries of history:

'The Scripture, foreseeing that God would justify the Gentiles by faith,
preached the Gospel beforehand unto Abraham, saying, In thee shall all
the nations be blessed' (Gal. 3. 8),

so that his Galatian converts are 'Abraham's seed, heirs according to
promise (3. 29).

ABRAHAM AND HISTORY

But we ask, Are the stories of Abraham, Isaac and Jacob real
history?

The answer that must be given is that pretty certainly Abraham
existed, and yet we have not reached the point where any of the
events can be dated; thus it is impossible to place at the head of this
chapter a list of the chief dates. On the other hand, as we shall see,

much of what we are told about Abraham, Isaac and Jacob is likely to have happened.

It is held as a definite conclusion that these narratives were not written down in a connected form till the reign of David or Solomon, that is, three hundred years or more after the Exodus, and much longer after Abraham. They were handed down by oral tradition; and though memories were retentive in the days before they were spoilt by reliance on written texts, those who told the stories were not interested in the sort of 'history' that is demanded by a modern History Professor. They were interested in their ancestral traditions, and interested also in speculating about the origin of their tribes; thus, Ishmael is connected with the Bedouin of Arabia, Esau with Edom, and Jacob with the twelve tribes of Israel. Still more, they were interested on the religious side, to see Abraham as the Man of Faith; this will come out strongly in our exposition. But even the mere historian finds some authentic historical material here.

First, we are told in Gen. 11. 28–31 that Abraham and his family, having originally come from Ur of the Chaldees in southern Mesopotamia, settled at Haran, in Padan-Aram (Gen. 28. 5–10), which was east of the Euphrates at the point where that river bends to the west and comes nearest to Syria; and it was from there that he came into Canaan, Gen. 12. 5. It is interesting to find that 'some of the names of the ancestors and family of Abraham were also names of towns in this area: that is, Peleg, Serug, Nahor and Terah' (*Westminster Bible Atlas*, p. 25: cf. Gen. 11. 16–24). So we find that Padan-Aram is the place to which Abraham sends to find a wife for Isaac, Gen. 24, and to which Jacob goes for the same purpose, 28. 1–5; it is the old family-home.

This tradition that Abraham came from beyond the Euphrates comes also in a liturgical form for the presentation of harvest-offerings to the LORD which dates from quite early in the life of the Israelites in Canaan, soon after the Conquest under Joshua, in Deuteronomy 26. 5–10. It begins, 'A wandering Aramaean was my father' (v. 5, R.V. margin); this is of course Abraham. Then it tells of the sojourn in Egypt, the oppression, and the Exodus and the Entry into Canaan. This is an instance of the 'Theology of

Recital' (cf. p. 14 above); the Israelite Creed is a remembering of the LORD's mighty acts. We get the same in Joshua 24. 2–15, at the Assembly of the Tribes at Shechem. Joshua's address to them begins with the Call of Abraham and his journey from 'beyond the River' to Canaan; it goes on to Isaac and Jacob, then Moses and the Deliverance from Egypt, and then the wanderings in the wilderness, the victories over the Amorites and the conquest of the land.

The traditions about Padan-Aram have lately been illustrated in a remarkable way by the excavations at Nuzi, which lies in the same region but considerably further east; it has been found that certain customs which appear in the patriarchal narratives but were not those of the Israelites at the time when the stories in Genesis were written down, correspond with those of the people of Nuzi. Some instances which are given are: the blessing pronounced by an old man before his death, cf. Genesis 27; the use of concubines to raise up heirs for the family, cf. Gen. 16. 1–3, and the relation between Abraham and Eliezer, who will become his heir if he has no child, Gen. 15. 1–4; and again, Esau's sale of his birthright, Gen. 25. 29–34. Other instances in the *Westminster Bible Atlas*, pp. 25 and 30, indicate that those stories preserve authentic memories. Yet again, the picture given in those stories of a semi-nomadic life in Palestine corresponds with the accounts which the archaeologists give of the condition of the country between 1700 and 1400 B.C. There is no reason to doubt the traditions which connect Abraham with Hebron, Isaac with Beersheba, and Jacob chiefly with Shechem. And finally, it can rightly be claimed that the portraits, especially of Abraham, are so life-like that they must surely rest on authentic memories.

It is not real history that we get in this part of the Book of Genesis, but there is historical material there. It is, however, the religious aspect of these chapters that is most important.

THE FAITH OF ABRAHAM

We have seen how Abraham, as a figure in history, has his place in some of the most ancient Recitals of Israel's faith, which correspond to our Creeds. The memory of Abraham as the Man of Faith has been treasured by his successors in the life of faith ever since.

So it was during the period when the stories about him were being handed down by oral tradition, before they were written down; and this will have been especially the case in the two centuries between Joshua's death and David's accession, from 1200 to 1000 B.C., when the Israelites, having entered Canaan after a period of nomadic life in the deserts, had to learn from their Canaanite neighbours the arts of agriculture. Necessarily therefore they learnt from the Canaanites the appropriate religious rites associated with ploughing and sowing and harvest. Hence came a great conflict, which could not be escaped, between the faith of the LORD the God of Israel and the nature-religions of Canaan, the cults of the Baalim and the Ashtaroth. The issue was this: Would the final result be that Israel's religion would be fundamentally Canaanite, with fragments of the religion of the LORD mixed in with it, so that he would become in effect one of the gods of the land, one of the Baals? Or would it be that the faith of the LORD who had redeemed them out of Egypt would remain dominant, and would incorporate into itself the positive elements of the Canaanite religion, so that he and he alone would be acknowledged as Israel's God, and be worshipped both as the Redeemer and as the God of nature and Lord of the harvest, the giver of the corn and the wine and the oil? They could be helped at this point by the picture which we have in Gen. 13, of Lot 'going Canaanite' when he went to live at Sodom though 'the men of Sodom were wicked and sinners against the LORD exceedingly' (Gen. 13. 13), while Abraham remained on the mountain at Hebron, waiting upon the LORD (vv. 14–18).

The faith of Abraham is referred to from time to time by the prophets (e.g. 1 Kings 18. 36, Isaiah 41. 8, 51. 2) and psalmists (e.g. Ps. 105. 6, 9), and by our Lord, as in Mark 12. 26. We have noticed in this chapter how to St. Paul Abraham is the man of faith, in Galatians ch. 3; and Romans ch. 4 is all about him. Then in Hebrews 11. 8ff. there is a glowing commentary on Gen. 12. 1–3:

'By faith Abraham, when he was called obeyed, to go out unto a place which he was to receive for an inheritance; and he went out, not knowing whither he went. By faith he became a sojourner in the land of promise, as in a land not his own, dwelling in tents, with Isaac and Jacob, the heirs with him of the same promise; for he looked for the City which hath foundations, whose builder and maker is God.'

We too today, for whom the whole future of our civilization is uncertain and who must expect to have to face great difficulties in our church life in the coming years, with great changes, certainly, in the outward shape of the Church, are being called by some of our leaders to take for our pattern the faith of Abraham, rather then, shall we say, that of Jeremiah, or of Nehemiah: 'our situation is Abraham's, and our integrity must be his too.'

The faith of Abraham throughout these chapters is faith in a God who makes promises concerning the future (12. 1–3, 7–8; 13. 14–18; 15. 1–6, and the rest of that chapter); we see how fundamental to the Old Testament is the conception of God as working out his purpose in history. Hence comes the preoccupation of Abraham with the birth of a son, his anxiety over the barrenness of Sarah (15. 2–3), and his willingness to obtain children by Hagar (16. 1–2), though he is told that God's purpose is not to be worked out this way (15. 4). Then in chapter 18 comes the word of the LORD that Sarah, in spite of her age, shall bear a son (18. 10). Sarah mocks at this, not believing that it can be true; but she is assured 'Is anything too hard for the LORD?' (18. 14). This word 'too hard for' ('*pala*') is one of the great words of the Bible; it comes again in the cognate word *niphla'oth*, which is variously translated as 'wondrous works', 'marvellous acts', and the like, as in Ps. 78. 12, 32, 43, where it refers to Israel's deliverance in the Exodus. It described the action of God in a situation where all human resources were at an end, and so was uniquely fitted for the occasion when Israel was in a seemingly hopeless case, caught between the pursuing Egyptian army and the Red Sea. Nothing is 'too hard for' the LORD if it is according to his will.

So Sarah's child is born. But after this comes the supreme trial of Abraham's faith, when the LORD 'tempts' (that is, 'proves' or 'tries' or 'tests') him by the command to offer him up in sacrifice:

'And it came to pass after these things, that God did prove Abraham, and said unto him, Abraham; and he said, Here am I. And he said, Take now thy son, thine only son, whom thou lovest, even Isaac, and get thee into the land of Moriah, and offer him there for a burnt-offering upon one of the mountains which I will tell thee of.' (Gen. 22. 1–2.)

Compared with such a demand, a command to an old man to surrender his own life would be a small thing. The command to offer up the son of the promise, with whom the whole future lies, seems the complete contradiction of the Purpose of God on which he has set his faith. Abraham in the story is called by God to make a supreme sacrifice, an act of complete and entire worship, trusting God in the dark, committing everything to him: 'not my will but thine be done'. While God did not in the end demand this sacrifice to be made, that which he did demand was the entire willingness to make the offering. Such is the meaning of the story as the writer tells it; and because this and nothing less is the true and original meaning therefore we, in interpreting it, may and must look onward to the self-giving of our LORD, in whose case no offering of a substitute was possible. Hence we may and must find the *final* answer to Isaac's question 'Where is the lamb for a burnt-offering?', and Abraham's reply 'God will provide himself the lamb for a burnt-offering, my son' (22. 7–8), in the words of John 1. 29 'Behold the Lamb of God that taketh away the sin of the world.'

The parallel with our Lord is suggested in Hebrews 11. 19, where it is said that in obeying the command to offer up Isaac, Abraham was

'accounting that God is able to raise up, even from the dead; from whence he did also in a parable receive him back.'

We are intended, as it seems, to think of our Lord, to whom it became clear that the divine Will for him was that he should offer himself in sacrifice, surrendering his life in the prime of life, with his life-work seemingly unaccomplished and ending in rejection by the People to whom he came; surrendering himself and his whole mission into the Father's hands. Such was the road which the Lord Jesus himself was content to tread. The way of God's Will led to a situation that was humanly impossible. He was vindicated when God raised him from the dead.

To the story of Abraham, Sarah and Isaac, there is added the episode of Hagar, the mother of Ishmael. Twice over, Hagar is sent into the desert, first when Sarah is jealous of her handmaid who has conceived (16. 5–6), and again after Isaac has been born and Hagar has mocked at him (21. 9–10). Yet each time we are told that God did not forget poor Hagar; in 16. 7–13 the Angel of the LORD finds her in the wilderness, and tells her that God has a purpose for Ishmael also, and (very movingly) again in 21. 14–21. after the water in the bottle is spent, and the mother has left the child to die:

'And the water in the bottle was spent, and she cast the child under one of the shrubs. And she went, and sat her down over against him a good way off, as it were a bowshot; for she said, Let me not look upon the death of the child. And she sat over against him, and lift up her voice and wept. And God heard the voice of the lad; and the Angel of God called to Hagar out of heaven, and said unto her, What aileth thee, Hagar? Fear not; for God hath heard the voice of the lad where he is. . . . And God opened her eyes, and she saw a well of water; and she went, and filled the bottle with water, and gave the lad drink.' (Gen. 21. 15–19.)

It would have been easy and natural for the writer, whose whole narrative turned on the working out of the Purpose through Isaac and not through Ishmael, to treat Hagar with indifference, as cast-off and rejected; was not Hagar's son Ishmael the ancestor of tribes who were constantly at war with Israel, and on whom God's vengeance was many times invoked (cf. Ps. 83. 6, 13–end)? But this is precisely what this writer will not do. He will not have his readers (or hearers) think of the surrounding pagan tribes as having nothing to do with God, or God with them.

The LORD was the God of the whole earth; and perhaps the writer intended to say to his contemporaries, 'When you go into Arabia or Egypt or Syria, do not imagine that you have gone out of the LORD's sight and beyond the range of his moral law; and do not despise the people there, because you belong to the LORD's chosen people.' And did not we in the days of British rule in Asia have a proverbial saying that one leaves the Ten Commandments behind when one goes east of Suez?

THE STORIES OF JACOB AND JOSEPH

About Isaac himself we are told little, but much about Jacob. He is presented as a highly unattractive character, at least in his early life; he manages in an underhand way to get Esau's birthright, and then he steals his blessing. And even though the story of the blessing establishes the dominance of Israel over Edom, its hated rival, yet it is so told as to make us sorry for Esau as the victim of Jacob's craftiness. It seems to be told as a character-study: Esau simply does not care about the birthright, the vocation and the promise (Gen. 25. 32–34), and he gets what he really cares about, an open-air life, chieftainship, wealth of flocks and herds, while Jacob, mean and deceitful though he is, yet is presented as a character that is ennobled through suffering. The writer who gave us the words, 'I will not leave thee, until I have done that which I have spoken to thee of' (28. 15), and who told of Jacob's fear after he had seen such a dream ('Surely the LORD is in this place, and I knew it not', v. 16), assuredly knew what divine vocation means. The bargaining spirit of his vow to the LORD on that occasion (if the LORD will be with him and look after him and bring him again to his home in peace, then he will take the LORD for his God and will duly pay him tithes, 28. 20–22) contrasts strongly with all that we are told about the faith of Abraham. But he has learnt his lesson by the time of his wrestling with God at Peniel (32. 24–30); and the writer who could tell the story which inspired Charles Wesley's great hymn, 'Come, O thou Traveller unknown' (*English Hymnal*, 378), knew what he was talking about. The Jacob of the later story, who sorrows for Joseph and Benjamin, is fit to be the ancestor of the twelve tribes of Israel.

The saga of Joseph is one that we can imagine as being recited to admiring and delighted audiences during the period when it was being handed down in the oral tradition. It is a fine narrative, brilliantly told; the recognition scene in ch. 44–45. 15 is a masterpiece. But there is more to it than this artistry of narrative; there are two high points in the story. The first is Joseph's moral uprightness in Potiphar's house, when he is all alone, with no prospects for his future, a slave in an Egyptian household, and he resists all his mistress' attempts to seduce him (ch. 39):

'Behold, my master knoweth not what is with me in the house, and he hath put all that he hath into my hand; there is none greater in this house than I, neither hath he kept back anything from me but thee, because thou art his wife: how then can I do this great wickedness, and sin against God?' (39. 8–9.)

The second is the climax to which the story leads up, which is the truth of the overruling by God of the selfish acts of evil men, when his brothers had sold him to the travelling merchants:

'As for you, ye meant much evil against me; but God meant it for good, to bring to pass as it is this day, to save much people alive.' (50. 20, cf. 45. 5–8.)

Plainly, the narrative as told is not straightforward 'history'; Jacob's sons would have needed more adequate transport arrangements than one ass and one sack each to supply the needs of the family for a long period (42, 25–27, 43, 1–2, etc.). Dr. Rowley seems to be right, in spite of the contrary view of Dr. Albright and the American scholars, in holding that Joseph's Pharaoh was none other than the great Akhnaton, who reigned from 1370 to 1353 B.C. and challenged the all-powerful priesthood of the god Amon on behalf of the (almost) monotheistic faith to which he had himself attained.

If this identification is right, it brings us to within a century of the Exodus.

CHAPTER IV

'Thy wonders of old time'

THE EXODUS AND THE ENTRY INTO CANAAN

Dates

Pharaoh Seti I	1319–1301
— Rameses II	1301–1234
— Merneptah	1235–1227
The Exodus	about 1280?
Entry into Canaan	1240?
Lachish captured	1221
League of the Tribes	1200?

GOD'S ACTION IN HISTORY

AFTER Genesis comes Exodus. Here we have the narrative of the events on which the existence of Israel as the People of God was based. They believed that the LORD their God, whom they felt and knew to be truly God in a sense in which the deities of the surrounding nations were not, had taken action in delivering them out of Egypt and uniting them to himself by a Covenant.

This sense of the reality of God does not mean merely that the Israelites had a somewhat more exalted conception of him than the other nations had of their gods. If that were all, we might expect to find the prophets exhorting the surrounding tribes to think more nobly of their gods, and saying that all the gods whom men worship are only names for the One. But they do not; they say the LORD is true God and the others are not, and they constantly refer back to the deliverance from Egypt (see, e.g. among the earliest prophets, Amos 2. 10, 3. 1–2; Hos. 2. 15, 11. 1; Mic. 6. 3–4). It is not that God does not care about other nations—for, says Amos, it is the LORD who has brought up the Philistines from Caphtor (probably Crete), and the Syrians from Kir, as well as Israel from the land of Egypt (Amos 9. 7)—it is that Israel stands in a unique position, in being called to belong to him who is the true God. In Deuteronomy the point is made and pressed home that the faith of Israel is an

39

altogether unique fact among the religions of the world, with no parallel anywhere else:

For ask now of the days that are past, which were before thee, since the day that God created man upon the earth, and from the one end of heaven unto the other, whether there hath been any such thing as this great thing is, or hath been heard like it? Did ever people hear the voice of God speaking out of the midst of the fire, as thou hast heard, and live? Or hath God assayed to go and take him a nation from the midst of another nation, by temptations, by signs, and by war, and by a mighty hand and a stretched out arm, and by great terrors, according to all that the LORD your God did for you in Egypt before your eyes? Unto thee it was shewed, that thou mightest know that the LORD he is God: there is none else beside him (Deut. 4. 32–35).

A faith such as the faith of old Israel in the God who redeemed it out of Egypt, or that of the Church in the Son of God come down from heaven, who was born as true man on earth, was crucified when Pontius Pilate was procurator of Judea, and rose victorious from death, makes an appeal to history which demands to be tested by the best methods of historical investigation. Only so can we answer the very legitimate question, whether these alleged events are not merely legendary; and if in fact the gospel records of the resurrection of our Lord can claim to be treated as the testimony of honest men to an amazing series of events, it is only historical criticism that can show this. And the Christian faith does depend on the answer, as St. Paul shows in 1 Cor. 15. 14–17. 'If Christ hath not been raised, then is our preaching vain, your faith also is vain. Yea, and we are found false witnesses of God, because we testified of God that he raised up Christ.' If it were proved beyond all reasonable doubt that Jesus of Nazareth never existed, but is a pure myth created by the religious needs of the world of that day; or that he was simply a teacher or religious reformer and no more, and that the whole claim that he was Messiah and Saviour was the invention of the Christian Church; or that the reliable historical record ends with his death, and the whole story of the resurrection is the product of wishful thinking on the part of disciples who dare not face facts—if any of these things were proved beyond reasonable doubt, the Christian

Faith would be at an end. For it stands on the assertion: 'Blessed be the God and Father of our Lord Jesus Christ, who according to his great mercy hath begotten us again unto a living hope by the resurrection of Jesus Christ from the dead' (1 Peter 1. 3).

The same must apply to the Old Testament, since there also it is proclaimed that God took action in a series of events in history.

THE EXODUS OF ISRAEL FROM EGYPT

The story of Israel as a nation begins with the Exodus from Egypt and the Covenant at Horeb. We do not need to take seriously the hypothesis that the whole narrative is mere myth, and there never was any Exodus at all; the historical evidence is too strong for that to be possible. What we do need to treat seriously is the hypothesis that there was indeed an Exodus under a great leader called Moses, but that this happened in a purely 'natural' way, and that it was later writers who first saw in it the work of such a God as the prophets believed in. On this hypothesis there was no true act of God in the Exodus.

The question we should now ask is, 'Of what character is the Exodus story, in the form in which it has come down to us?' If it was a traditional story that was radically changed so that it came to mean something entirely different, the Exodus-story will have been originally a folk-tale telling of the glory and prowess of Israel's God, his might in overthrowing his enemies, and the prowess of his people too as they fight their battles under his leadership and protection; and some traces of this view would assuredly persist in the story, after it had been re-written.

Certainly the power of the LORD is shown in the repeated plagues of Egypt, and above all in the overwhelming of the Egyptian army in the Red Sea. But we shall expect to hear of Israel's prowess also. Do we find this? Instead, we find Moses' act in killing the Egyptian and rescuing the Hebrew (Exod. 2. 11–12) not accepted with gratitude as by a noble race longing for its deliverance (2. 13–14). Moses at Horeb receives the revelation of God's Name, and the call to go and deliver Israel (3. 1–14); yet Moses, the great Moses, shrinks from the task and does all he can to escape from it (4. 1–17), before at last he goes. The first plea to Pharaoh, that he let the people go, produces only an increase of the people's burdens, and they tell Moses that they do not want his promised deliverance; they are better as they are, and prefer to remain in slavery (5. 21). After this, the Plagues of Egypt follow, culminating in the Passover and the passage of the Red Sea. This is the very hour of deliverance; yet the Israelites are not represented as a band of brave men fighting their way through to freedom, nor as dying like the Spartans at Thermopylae, but as a herd of helpless fugitives, caught between the sea and their enemies, and expecting next morning a fate worse than death, and saying to Moses,

Because there were no graves in Egypt, hast thou taken us away to die in the wilderness? . . . Is not this the word that we spake unto thee in Egypt, 'Let us alone, that we may serve the Egyptians'? (14. 11–12.)

Yet they came through. It has been suggested that there was a volcanic eruption further down the Red Sea, so that the water receded and the Israelites, seeing dry ground before them in the light of the paschal moon, hurried across; then the Egyptians following them were engulfed in the immense tidal wave which came in when the waters returned. But this is only a theory; and it seems more likely that neither Moses nor the Israelites understood exactly what had happened. It does appear however that the sight that they saw is recorded in the very ancient ballad of Exodus 15:

I will sing to the LORD, for he hath triumphed gloriously,
The horse and his rider hath he thrown into the sea.

This is nothing even remotely like the ordinary patriotic tale, which glorifies at once the tribal god, the heroic leader, and the people. There is emphasis on the slowness even of the great leader to accept his mission, and on the servility and timidity of the people, entirely unlike the praises of their prowess that we get in the Song of Deborah in Judges 5; and this attitude on the part of the people can be no later addition to the story, for it is on the helplessness of the people in the hour of their deliverance that the whole record hangs. We may remind ourselves that the same feature appears in the narratives of our Lord's passion, where we are told, not how the faithful disciples stood by their Lord to the last, but how 'they all forsook him and fled', and one of them betrayed him and one disowned him publicly. Here the apostles, who are proclaiming to the world that Christ died to save sinners, are heard confessing their own share in the common sin. Both in the New Testament and in the Old Testament instance, when the usual human tendency to self-congratulation and self-praise is thus reversed, the inference is that some real event has happened to produce such a phenomenon.

In chapters 4–11 of the Book of Deuteronomy, written towards the end of the pre-exilic period, we get a series of magnificent homilies on the Exodus and the vocation of Israel which results from it.

Here is a notable piece of commentary:

Thou art a holy people unto the LORD thy God: the LORD thy God hath chosen thee to be a peculiar people to himself, above all peoples that are on the face of the earth. The LORD did not set his love upon you nor choose you, because ye were more in number than any people: for ye were the fewest of all peoples: but because the LORD loveth you, and because he would keep the oath which he sware unto your fathers, hath the LORD brought you out with a mighty hand, and redeemed you out of the house of bondage, from the hand of Pharoah king of Egypt. (Deut. 7. 6–8.)

The nation which the LORD chose to be his people was a small and insignificant nation. (Here we may note that the figure of 'six hundred thousand men that drew sword, besides women and children' in Exod. 12, 37 belongs to a later version of the story; the actual number may have been a few thousands all told.) The general sense of the Deuteronomic interpretation is true to that of the narrative in Exodus, where the LORD God is praised for the amazing deliverance at the Red Sea and Moses the great leader is shown as his unworthy human instrument, and the people as the unworthy objects of his mercy.

Nor did Israel make up for the smallness of its numbers by the high quality of its devotion. Repeatedly Israel in the wilderness is found 'murmuring against Moses and against God' (Exod. 15. 24; 16. 2, 7: Num. 20. 2–13). Here is another Deuteronomic commentary:

D

Thou shalt remember all the way that the LORD thy God hath led thee these forty years in the wilderness, that he might humble thee, to prove thee, to know what was in thine heart, whether thou wouldst keep his commandments, or no. And he humbled thee, and suffered thee to hunger, and fed thee with manna, which thou knewest not, neither did thy fathers know, that he might make thee know that man doth not live by bread alone, but by every thing that proceedeth out of the mouth of the LORD doth man live. (Deut. 8. 2–3.)

The rest of this chapter, and the following chapters, enlarge on the theme that it was the same after the people entered Canaan. There was to be the danger

lest when thou hast eaten and art full, and hast built goodly houses and dwelt therein, and when thy herds and thy flocks multiply, and thy silver and thy gold is multiplied, and all that thou hast is multiplied, then thine heart be lifted up and thou forget the LORD thy God, which brought thee forth out of the land of Egypt, out of the house of bondage. (Duet. 8. 12–14.)

Israel having received its vocation had still to make good.

THE COVENANT

To return now from Deuteronomy to Exodus: we read in chapter 24 of a solemn sacrifice with communion feast, at which the Covenant of the LORD with Israel was ratified and sealed, and Israel was consecrated to him.

The ordinary sort of 'covenant' was a bargain or pact between one man and another, by which the two parties entered on a new relation, with reciprocal rights and duties. Such is the covenant of Jacob and Laban in Gen. 31. 44–45. Here the two parties stand on an equal footing. But when God makes a covenant with men, the two parties do not stand on an equal footing. Such a covenant cannot therefore be thought of as a species of bargain, but must rest on the gracious mercy of God, condescending to enter on a relation with men, and admitting men to a special relation to him. It is therefore entirely misleading and wrong to represent his Covenant with Israel as an agreement or contract, so that if man fails to perform his duty to God, the Covenant is broken. On the contrary: the Covenant stands, even when Israel sins, because its basis is the free act of the divine Love, as in Deut. 7. 6–8, quoted on page 43 above. Another expression of the idea is the relation of Bridegroom and Bride, which we meet in the prophet Hosea (see pp. 64–65 below); as Hosea still loved his unfaithful wife, so the LORD still loves sinful Israel.

There are also Covenants with God *made by men*, when in some special situation men remind themselves of the Covenant which God has made with them, and undertake to perform their own duty to him. Such is the Covenant which Joshua and the tribes assembled at Shechem make in Josh. 24. 22–25, as we shall see later on in this chapter, and that of king Josiah on the occasion of the acceptance of the Deuteronomic Law (2 Kings 23. 3, see p. 70 below). But the primary Covenant is that of Sinai, when the LORD takes Israel for his chosen people, and when they receive the Ten Commandments.

There is every reason to think that the Ten Commandments really were given by Moses. They are set out in two places, Exod. 20. 1–17 and Deut. 5. 6–21. In both versions there are commentaries on some of the Commandments, namely II, III, IV, V and X, which in the case of IV and X are widely different; but I, VI, VII, VIII and IX consist of one short sentence only, and it is probable that all the Commandments as originally given were in this form, for the two versions are identical, except for one word in Commandment IV. Both versions begin with the words

'I am the LORD thy God, which brought thee out of the land of Egypt, out of the house of bondage': (therefore)

I.   'Thou shalt have none other gods but me.'
II.   'Thou shalt not make to thyself any graven image.'
III.   'Thou shalt not take the Name of the LORD thy God in vain.'
IV.   'Remember (*or* Observe) the Sabbath day to keep it holy.'
V.   'Honour thy father and thy mother.'
VI.   'Thou shalt do no murder.'
VII. 'Thou shalt not commit adultery.'
VIII. 'Thou shalt not steal.'
IX.   'Thou shalt not bear false witness against thy neighbour.'
X.   'Thou shalt not covet.'

The Commandments are likely to be Mosaic, for they fit the situation at that time. I–IV speak of Israel's duty to the God to whom it owed unbounded gratitude and worship, for its deliverance from Egypt; and V–X give man's duty to his neighbour, since the Israelites, who had suffered cruel wrong from their fellow-men in Egypt, must now learn to behave rightly to their fellow-men. Here the Ten Commandments stand in sharp contrast with the other codes of law attributed to Moses; for these all presuppose a settled life in an agricultural community, as does for instance the so-called Book of the Covenant, Exod. 20. 22–23. 19, while later codes call for elaborate craftsmanship in metal-working and embroidery and setting of jewels, as in Exod. 25–30.

All the Laws are called 'Laws of Moses', just as the Psalms are 'Psalms of David' because psalmody had its beginning with David, and Proverbs and most of the other 'Wisdom books' (pp. 59, 111 below) are attributed to Solomon because he was renowned for his wisdom. So it is with the Law; Israel's Law did in fact begin with the Ten Commandments given by Moses, and Moses was always looked to as the fountain-head, on the human side, of the Law. It had indeed been the LORD's work and his alone, to deliver Israel out of Egypt and take it to be his people. But Moses had been the leader in the Exodus, and his part had been to interpret, by the Spirit, what the LORD was doing with them, and so to be the mediator of the Covenant, and draw forth from the people their response of love and obedience. Hence in the concluding paragraph of the Pentateuch, Deut. 34. 10–12, Moses is called the greatest of all the prophets:

'There hath not arisen a prophet since in Israel like unto Moses, whom the LORD knew face to face.'

THE CONQUEST OF CANAAN

Yet Moses himself did not lead the people into the Promised Land. There was a whole generation, according to the tradition, of wanderings in the wilderness, and of this we have only fragmentary accounts, chiefly in the Book of Numbers, 10. 11 to ch. 24, and in

Deut. 1–3. The tradition is quite definite that the main body of the Israelites entered Canaan from the east, across the Jordan, after victorious battles against Sihon and Og; these were always remembered, and are alluded to several times in the Psalms.

Some chapters in the Book of Joshua give the impression that Joshua effected a sweeping conquest of the whole country. But it is clear from some other places in that book and in Judges ch. 1, that there were many important fortresses which the Israelites were then unable to take (see Josh. 15. 63, 16. 10, 17. 11–12; Judges 1. 10, 11–15 and 21. 27, 29). The Book of Joshua does describe a successful campaign westwards from Jericho, with a big battle at Beth-horon, ch. 10, and another in the far north, beyond the Sea of Galilee, when Hazor, described as 'the head of all those kingdoms', ch. 11. 1–15, was taken. Both these campaigns have been verified by the work of the archaeologists in the last thirty years; the sites of Bethel, Lachish, Debir and Eglon have been excavated, and it seems to be proved that Lachish was taken about 1220 B.C., and that all these cities fell to invaders who were on a markedly lower level of civilization than those whom they dispossessed. This is shown by the use which the invaders made of the captured cities. Similarly in the far north, Hazor has been excavated since 1955 by an Israeli expedition led by Dr. Yigael Yadin, and there is good reason to think that it was Joshua who took this place, which was the largest city then existing in Canaan.

But there is no mention of any campaign in central Palestine, round about Shechem; and since this was always a very important part of the country, this would be most surprising, unless that part of the country was already in Israelite hands. It is generally held that this was the case, and that there had been Israelites there since the time of the patriarchs, who had not gone down into Egypt and had not shared in the Exodus.

THE LEAGUE OF THE TRIBES

It was for this reason, as it seems, that Joshua called an Assembly of all the Tribes at Shechem, as is described in Joshua 24. Joshua in his address to them reminds them of what they know already, about their origin from Abraham and his journey to Canaan from beyond the Euphrates, in obedience to the LORD's call. Then he tells them what some of them do not know, about the Sojourn in Egypt, the Oppression, the Deliverance in the Exodus, and what had happened since then. Then he asks them whether they will accept this faith in the LORD their Deliverer, and he makes it clear that it is no light thing that he is asking of them; it means that they must renounce the nature-religions of Canaan, like Abraham who after his Call came to him from the LORD, had served him. The people answer that they will; and so they make a Covenant together, promising to live as the People of the LORD.

So the League of the Tribes was formed, which lasted for a century and a half from about 1200 to 1050 B.C. There were regular festivals, when they 'appeared before the LORD', first at Shechem and later at Shiloh. This was the period of the 'Judges', the Judge being not in the first place an administrator of the law, but rather a chieftain who arose in the LORD's Name to call the tribes together to repel some invasion of the land. There was one such rally of the tribes under Deborah and Barak, which was the occasion of the great ballad in Judges 5, the earliest complete Hebrew poem that we possess, when the invasion of Sisera from the north was repelled. Another was the rally under Gideon, related in Judges 6-8, when Midianites from the desert had crossed the Jordan and ravaged the sown lands.

The League of the Tribes was thus a loose confederation; as yet there was no permanent king. The Israelites were evidently far from faithful to the Covenant which they had made with Joshua; settled on their farms, they were continually falling back into the ways of their Canaanite neighbours, and serving the Baalim and the Ashtaroth. But when the Judges arose to lead them into battle, they realized again their national unity, and that they were in truth the People of the LORD.

We shall see in the next chapter how a far greater peril to the nation's life arose from the Philistine invasions, and how the place of the Judge had to be taken by a King.

CHAPTER V

'I have found David My Servant'

DAVID AND THE MONARCHY

Dates

Arrival of the Philistines	about 1180
Shiloh destroyed	1050
Saul's reign	1020–1004
David king at Hebron	1004
David king over all Israel	998–965

THE PHILISTINES

THE League of the Tribes was adequate to repel invasions from the desert; but it broke down when the Philistines had established themselves in the coastal plain opposite the territory of Judah, and after building their cities and becoming settled in, began to invade the hill-country. It was a very critical situation indeed for Israel when they took Shiloh and destroyed it about 1050 B.C. (as the excavation of the site has proved), and again when Saul was defeated and killed with his two sons some forty-five years later.

The Philistines were not Semites; Amos says that they came from Caphtor (Crete), which was a flourishing centre of the civilization which preceded that of the Greeks. They tried first to settle in the Nile delta, soon after 1200 B.C., but were defeated by the Egyptians in what seems to be the first naval battle of which we have record; then they settled 150 miles further to the east. The Iron Age was beginning, and they jealously guarded the secret of working in iron, as we see in 1 Samuel 13. 19–22. Yet they did not succeed in subjugating the Israelites completely; perhaps the reason was that they were organized as a federation of five cities, Gaza, Ashdod, Askelon, Gath and Ekron, and never had a really unified government.

A League which depended on the voluntary co-operation of widely scattered tribes could not stand against such an attack, and the only hope lay in a monarchy. We have two accounts of the rise

of King Saul to power: an earlier account in 1 Sam. 9, 10. 1–16, and
11, and a later one in chs. 8, 10. 17–27 and 12. This later account
stresses the spiritual danger to Israel in having 'a king like all the
nations' (1 Sam. 8. 5), and in becoming a civilized and fully organized nation; what would happen to the freedom which Israel had
enjoyed under the tribal system, and to the common relation of the
tribes to the LORD? But the risk had to be accepted; and it was the
work of David to organize a United Israel, bringing into unity the
Judah-tribes in the south and the central and northern tribes led by
Ephraim.

In the preliminary stages of this re-organization Samuel, the last
of the 'Judges', took a leading part, and it was he who made Saul
king. Saul was a brave and generous leader, patriotic and devoted.
He had his headquarters at the little town of Gibeah, some five miles
north of Jerusalem, and it is clear that his was a very rustic 'court';
when the summons comes in ch. 11. 4–6 that the town of Jabesh
across the Jordan is in desperate straits from an attack by the Am-
monites, he is busy ploughing his fields, and he sends out a call to
the tribes like one of the Judges. But Samuel sees that he has got
to be king.

It is difficult to assess Saul's character; our accounts all come from
the partisans of David his rival and successor. He was a brave
leader, but it is clear that there was a neurotic strain in him; 'an
evil spirit from the LORD troubled him' (1 Sam. 16. 14, 18. 10, 19. 9),
and he broke down badly at the very end when he consulted the
witch of Endor (ch. 28. 3–25).

He had some considerable success in resisting the Philistines, and
it is in the course of these compaigns that David comes on the scene
as a young man of great promise. Saul did hold the Israelite forces
together, though when, as we find in ch. 14, the enemy were oc-
cupying Michmash, they were across the central ridge of the
country; later on they held Bethlehem (2 Sam. 23. 14), at the time
when David was in flight from Saul; and after Saul's defeat and
death the whole of the country was at their mercy.

DAVID HIMSELF

David's life falls into four periods: (i) when as a young man he is serving under Saul; (ii) when the breach with Saul is complete and he is an outlaw; (iii) when he has been anointed as king in the Judahite city of Hebron; and (iv) when he is king in Jerusalem as the capital of United Israel. Conveniently enough for us, the date when he became king is about 1000 B.C.

David was a born leader of men, and throughout his life he inspired the most devoted loyalty. Personally he was most attractive, with beautiful eyes (this is the literal meaning of 'of a beautiful countenance', 1 Sam. 16. 12). He was able to lead and to control at the cave of Adullam a motley crowd of 'everyone who was in distress, or in debt, or discontented', 22. 2. There was one specially difficult moment shortly before Saul's death, when in the absence of David and the fighting men, some Amalekites had raided Ziklag and carried off the men's wives and children and cattle, and they talked of stoning David, 29.6; but he was equal to the occasion, and organized a pursuing party which recovered the captives, and he made those whom he had taken with him in the pursuit share the spoils with those who had been left behind, 29. 7–25.

There was a whole sheaf of stories about the beloved leader. Once when he had been very nearly killed in battle with a giant Philistine and just rescued in time by Abishai, they all said that he must not go into battle himself 'that thou quench not the lamp of Israel' (2 Sam. 21. 15–17). Another time, when he was at Adullam and had expressed a longing desire to drink from the well at Bethlehem, three of his young men made their way past the Philistine garrison and drew some water from that well and brought it to him to drink. David would not drink it, but poured it out as a drink-offering to the LORD, saying, 'Far be it from me to drink it! Shall I drink the blood of my men that went in jeopardy of their lives?' (2 Sam. 23. 14–17). The stories of his chivalry to Saul when he spared his life (1 Sam. 24 and 26) are well known; and in ch. 25 there is the thrilling story of Abigail the wife of the wealthy but churlish Nabal. Then there is of course the story of David and Goliath in 1 Sam. 17;

we all want to think that it was David who did it, but unfortunately
2 Sam. 21. 19 tells us that Goliath was killed by someone else.
Perhaps however 1 Sam. 17 is right, after all.

David could come out on top in a very difficult situation. While
he was king at Hebron, Abner, who had been the commander on
behalf of Saul's son in the little local war against David, but who
had seen the vision of a United Israel and had come to negotiate
with David about it, had been treacherously murdered by Joab on
account of a family blood-feud (2 Sam. 3. 6–27); what now was
David to do? He publicly repudiated Joab's act, and walked as the
chief mourner at Abner's funeral, and refused to touch any food
for the whole day till sundown:

'... and all the people took notice of it, and it pleased them, as whatsoever
the king did pleased all the people. So all the people, and all Israel,
understood that it was not of the king to slay Abner the son of Ner'
(2 Sam. 3. 35–37).

After this it was possible for there to be a United Israel.

When the union had been effected, and Jerusalem had been
captured and made the capital, there followed an astonishing series
of victories: over the Philistines, who from now on were confined
to the coastal plain, and also over Moab and Ammon to the south-
east, Ammon to the east, and Syria as far as beyond Damascus—all
these made up a small empire. David was victorious everywhere.
We must not put down these successes only to his strategical and
tactical skill, but still more to the loyalty and enthusiasm of the
fighting men. In this Elizabethan age of Israel's history, nothing
seemed to be impossible.

It was an Elizabethan Age also in the literary output which it
produced; for it was now that the Books of Genesis and Exodus
began to be written in their earliest forms. It was not for nothing
that David was always thought of afterwards as *the* king of Israel.

DAVID AS STATESMAN

David's political problem was that of bringing together the
southern and northern tribes into one nation, and overcoming their
long-standing alienation.

The southern and northern tribes had been brought together in the League of the Tribes under Joshua. But during the period of the Judges, Judah was too far away to take part in the two great rallies of the Tribes under Deborah and under Gideon; it is not mentioned in Judges 5 and 6–7. Probably free intercourse was hindered by the existence of two Canaanite fortresses between Judah and Ephraim: Jerusalem, which was taken by David, 2 Sam. 5. 6–10, and Gezer, which was not taken till Solomon's reign, 1 Kings 9. 16. The north did not take kindly to a king from Judah, till Abner persuaded them and David won their hearts; but they shared fully in the glory of David's reign. Yet it seems that even David did not fully see the importance of keeping the loyalty and goodwill of the northern tribes.

This emerges from the history of David's reign in 2 Sam. 10–20. The same writer may have been responsible for much of the earlier history of David; and scholars seem to agree that we have here a contemporary document, written while the memory of the events was fresh, by a great historian who had a keen insight into the greatness of David and his partial failure.

David's greatness comes out in the story of Absalom's rebellion, as when the two priests carried out the Sacred Ark to go with David —for the Ark had always gone with the army to battle, as we see in 2 Sam. 11. 11—but David saw that while the Ark was the symbol of the LORD's presence, it was not an idol; and so he said to them:

'Carry back the Ark of God into the city. If I find favour in the eyes of the LORD, he will bring me again and show me both it and his habitation; but if he say thus, I have no delight in thee, behold, here am I, let him do what seemeth good unto him' (2 Sam. 15. 25–26).

David was also great enough not to let himself be troubled by the cursings of Shimei (16. 5–14).

But our historian shows another side to the picture. It begins with his act of adultery with Bathsheba, 'at the return of the year, at the time when kings go out to battle' (2 Sam. 11. 1)—ought David to have been with the army at the front, instead of sitting in comfort at home? Then comes the story of his thoroughly mean behaviour

towards Uriah the Hittite, 11. 14–21; and then the better side, his
confession of his guilt to the prophet Nathan: 'I have sinned against
the LORD', 12. 1–13.

There was not only the sin with Bathsheba; there was also his
polygamy, the result of which was that he had many sons by different
mothers, so that he was unable to control them. We are told in
ch. 13 of Amnon's outrage against his half-sister Tamar, and the
fierce revenge of Absalom who was Tamar's brother, and then of
Absalom's flight into exile; and yet, while the king grieved over
Absalom, he did nothing to bring him back till Joab, loyal in spite of
all, found a clever way of gaining this end; yet even so, David would
not see him (14. 1–24).

Our historian says of Absalom that 'in all Israel there was none
so much praised as Absalom, and from the sole of his foot to the
crown of his head there was no blemish in him', 14. 25—does he
suggest that Absalom ought to have been David's successor on the
throne, and that David, who was now getting old, might have
trusted this promising son with responsibility? For in 15. 1–5 we
find Absalom pointing out that David is not doing his duty in
providing for legal cases to be heard, so that people might get
justice; and we find him yielding to the temptation to conspire
against his father, till in 15. 7–12 he gets himself anointed as king in
Hebron. ('Forty years', 15. 7, is a mistake for 'four'.) The story of
the rebellion of Absalom follows.

At the end of it comes another failure on David's part; he fails to
see the importance of keeping on the right side of the northern
tribes, who always remembered that David came from Judah. When
the men of Israel are talking of bringing the king back, 19. 8–10,
David turns instead to his own kinsfolk of Judah, 19. 11–15, at
the same time humiliating the loyal Joab, 19. 5–8 and 13; there is
then a heated argument between the men of Israel and the men of
Judah, which augurs ill for the future, 19. 40–43. In ch. 20 another
rebellion follows, that of Sheba the son of Bichri, which Joab over-
comes without difficulty, 20. 13–22; but the ominous thing here is
that Sheba's war-cry, 'We have no portion in David, neither have
we inheritance in the son of Jesse: every man to his tents, O Israel'

(20. 1), is repeated word for word in 1 Kings 12. 16, when the final disruption of the kingdom takes place under Jeroboam.

Thus, while David achieved the union of the south and the north in one kingdom, our historian shows that the seeds of the fatal disruption had been already sown in David's reign.

THE COVENANT WITH DAVID

In this account of David's faults as a statesman, too little has been said of the moral and religious ideals which he set before himself as king. David saw that as the LORD is righteous, so the king who rules in subordination to him as 'the LORD's Anointed', must rule in righteousness. This is set out in a beautiful poem attributed to David in 2 Sam. 23. 1–7, which can well be the work of David himself; it is certainly worthy of the author of the 'Lament over Saul and Jonathan' in 2 Sam. 1. 19–27. (Notice that in reading 2 Sam. 23. 1–7 in the R.V., it is necessary to accept the marginal rendering in two places.)

'The God of Israel said,
  The Rock of Israel spoke to me:
"One that ruleth over men righteously,
  That ruleth in the fear of God,
He shall be as the light of the morning,
    When the sun riseth,
A morning without clouds,
    When the tender grass springeth out of the earth,
    Through clear shining after rain."
For is not my house so with God?
For he hath made with me an everlasting Covenant,
    Ordered in all things, and sure.
For all my salvation and all my desire,
Will he not make it to grow?

But the ungodly shall be all of them as thorns to be thrust away
For they cannot be taken with the hand,
But the man that toucheth them
Must be armed with iron and the staff of a spear,
And they shall be utterly burned with fire in their place.'

The king must rule righteously. Dr. Aubrey Johnson has shown in his book *Sacral Kingship in Ancient Israel* that David may have first put the idea into words when he captured Jerusalem and found there a venerable sanctuary of *El Elyon* ('God Most High') with a tradition of a priest-king Melchizedek. *Melek* means 'king' and *ẓedek* 'righteousness'; the name *Melchiẓedek* means, 'My King is righteous' ('King' being thus a Divine name), just as the name 'Zedekiah' means 'the LORD is righteous'. The names *El Elyon* and *Melchiẓedek* come in Gen. 14. 18–20; this chapter is quite unlike those which come before and after it in the Book of Genesis, and it is believed that David may have been responsible for seeing that this chapter, derived from the old Jerusalem sanctuary, was preserved in the J-narrative, which is now held to date from David's reign or Solomon's. The temple-rock at Jerusalem, which was the site of the great altar in Solomon's temple, was bought by David, not confiscated, from Araunah the Jebusite (2 Sam. 24. 18–24).

The theme of the king ruling in righteousness reappears in a number of Psalms which speak of the LORD as King, or of the Davidic king, and are regarded by modern scholars as belonging to the Autumn Festival for the blessing of the king and his kingdom, with prayers for rain and for the prosperity which a good harvest would bring. One of these is Ps. 72:

'Give the king thy judgements, O God,
And righteousness unto the king's son.
He shall judge thy people with righteousness,
And thy poor with judgement . . .
He shall come down like rain upon the mown grass,
As showers that water the earth.
In his days shall the righteous flourish,
And abundance of peace, till the moon be no more (Ps. 72, 1–2, 6–7).

Then success is promised him, and world-wide rule far exceeding the empire of David, and anything that could be prayed for or expected in the ordinary course of things, for a king of Israel:

'All kings shall fall down before him;
All nations shall serve him . . .
His name shall endure for ever;

His name shall be continued as long as the sun;
All nations shall be blessed in him,
All nations shall call him happy' (vv. 11, 17).

As Dr. Aubrey Johnson has seen, the psalmist is looking forward
beyond the actual kingdom of David and his successors, to a
Future Kingdom in which God's purpose for Israel will be complete, to a Kingdom of which David's reign had given a glimpse.

This becomes clear in Ps. 89, in which verses 3–4 and the
middle section, 19–37, are about the LORD's Covenant with David:

'I have found David my servant;
With my holy oil have I anointed him . . .
He shall cry to me, "Thou art my Father,
My God, and the Rock of my salvation".
I also will make him my first-born,
Higher than the kings of the earth' (vv. 20, 26–27).

There could be, and there were, bad kings of David's line:

'If his children forsake my law,
And walk not in my judgements,
If they break my statutes and keep not my commandments,
Then I will visit their transgressions with the rod,
And their iniquity with stripes' (vv. 30–32).

But even so, the LORD's purpose will stand:

'But my mercy will I not utterly take from him,
Nor suffer my faithfulness to fail.
My Covenant will I not break,
Nor alter the thing that is gone out of my lips.
Once have I sworn by my holiness,
I will not lie unto David:
His seed shall endure for ever,
And his throne as the sun before me.
It shall be established for ever as the moon,
And as the faithful witness in the sky' (vv. 33–37).

Thus in spite of human unfaithfulness the LORD would establish at
last the throne of his Messiah, his Anointed King.

It seems possible that this hope of an ideal Future Kingdom really
was held by David himself, even though many of these psalms of

the Kingship were probably composed for the Royal Festival during the period between David and the Exile. The two great prophecies of the Davidic King in Isa. 9. 1–7 and 11. 1–10 must surely belong to that Festival:

'For unto us a child is born,
  Unto us a son is given;
  And the government shall be upon his shoulder.
  And his name shall be called
    Wonderful, Counsellor,
    Mighty God,
    Everlasting Father,
    Prince of Peace,
Of the increase of his government and of peace there shall be no end,
Upon the throne of David and upon his kingdom . . .' (9. 6–7).

The king is to be filled with the Spirit of the LORD:

'There shall come forth a shoot out of the stock of Jesse,
  And a branch out of his roots shall bear fruit:
And the Spirit of the LORD shall rest upon him,
    The Spirit of wisdom and understanding,
    The Spirit of counsel and might,
    The Spirit of knowledge and of the fear of the LORD;
And his delight shall be in the fear of the LORD:
And he shall not judge after the sight of his eyes,
Neither reprove after the hearing of his ears
But with righteousness shall he judge the poor,
And reprove with equity for the meek of the earth . . . (11. 1–4).

In 587 B.C. the Davidic Monarchy ceased to exist, and with it the Royal Festival. But the psalms and the prophecies continued in use; and though Israel was for centuries a subject people under the Babylonian, Persian and Greek empires, the Hope still lived of a future King, the LORD's Anointed, the Messiah, the Christos (for these three are one word, in English, Hebrew and Greek), till right at the end of the Old Testament period the slumbering Hope awoke to life—as we shall see at the end of chapter X. In chapter XI we shall see how it found its true Fulfilment.

CHAPTER VI

'O Israel, what shall I do unto thee?'

THE DIVIDED KINGDOM, AND THE PROPHETIC MESSAGE

Dates

Solomon's reign	965–926
Omri	882–871
Ahab his son	871–852
Jeroboam II	787–747
Fall of Samaria	721

In Judah

Jehoshaphat	872–852
Athaliah	845–839
Ahaz	742–725
Hezekiah	725–697
Manasseh	696–642
Josiah	639–609

Prophets:

Amos, in the reign of Jeroboam II; Hosea, perhaps 20 years later. Isaiah, 740 till after 701; Micah, perhaps from about 740 onwards.

THE DISRUPTION

WITHIN forty years after David's death, the disastrous disruption of the kingdom had taken place; the hope that Israel might meet the new problems of civilized life as a united nation had broken down. David had been a great king, but had also had great faults. What do we say of Solomon?

Solomon was greatly honoured in later times in Israel, first as the Man of Wisdom. He was famed for this is his life-time, as we see in the story of his dream, 1 Kings 3. 4–15, and of his wisdom in giving judgement, 3. 16–28, his proverbs and songs, 4. 29–34, and the visit of the Queen of Sheba, 11. 1–10. Later, the Books of Proverbs and Ecclesiastes and the Song of Songs, and in the Apocrypha the

Wisdom of Solomon, were attributed to him. He was no less greatly honoured as the Temple-builder; his splendid temple became at once a centre of Israel's religion, and became increasingly important when it had come to be the one place where sacrifice could be offered (see p. 71 below); after its destruction at the Fall of Jerusalem the returned exiles made it their first object to rebuild it. After that, it was regarded by every Jew as the spiritual centre of the world, and in Rev. 21 St. John sees the 'New Jerusalem' as the symbol of Heaven itself.

But there was another side to the picture. Solomon son of Bathsheba had been born in a palace and had known nothing of the heroic period of David's life; he had also grown up in a polygamous household, and he became the great polygamist of history (1 Kings 11. 1–8). Those of his wives who were foreign princesses required sanctuaries to be built for the worship of their gods; so 'his wives turned away his heart'. Then again, Solomon was the Millionaire-king, receiving the immense annual income of 666 talents of gold (10. 14) from trade and customs-dues on trade routes (9. 26–28, 10. 11–12, 22–29). The country was divided into taxation districts (4. 7–20), and the people into labour-gangs (5. 13–18); and when the northern tribes revolted against his son, the first thing that they did was to seize Adoram the Minister of Labour, and to 'stone him with stones, that he died' (12. 18). Hence the Law of the King in Deut. 18. 14–20 says with the greatest plainness that the king is not to 'multiply horses to himself', nor to 'multiply wives to himself'; neither shall he greatly multiply to himself silver and gold'. There must not be another Solomon.

The political disruption involved also schism, when Jeroboam felt himself compelled to institute a rival Autumn Festival at Bethel:

'And Jeroboam said in his heart, Now shall the kingdom return to the house of David, if this people go up to offer sacrifices in the house of the LORD at Jerusalem; then shall the heart of this people turn again unto their lord, even unto Rehoboam king of Judah, and they shall kill me and return to Rehoboam king of Judah' (12. 26–27).

So the Judaean writer expresses it; and he directly compares the Golden Calves to the Calf made by Aaron at Sinai, since the words

'Behold thy gods, O Israel, which brought thee out of the land of Egypt' vs. 28) are identical with the words used in Exodus 32. 4 and 8.

Politically, the result of the Disruption was disastrous; Israel and Judah were frequently engaged in futile wars, and so were Israel and Syria, in spite of the growing menace from the militarism of the Assyrian Empire. We know from an Assyrian inscription that at the Battle of Karkar in 853 King Ahab led a strong contingent in the allied army of the free nations, which in that battle decisively checked Assyrian aggression for the time being; yet within two years Israel and Syria were fighting again at Ramoth-gilead (1 Kings 22).

There came also a new peril to Israel's religion. Omri, who was a strong and great king (882–871), and built the splendid capital city of Samaria, married his son Ahab to Jezebel, a princess from Tyre; and this masterful queen introduced the cult of the Tyrian Baal on a large scale. It was against this peril to Israel's faith that the prophet Elijah contended. Athaliah, Omri's granddaughter and so probably Jezebel's daughter (2 Kings 8. 26), brought the same peril to Judah when as the queen-mother after king Ahaziah's death (11. 1) she tried to blot out the Davidic line of kings; but Ahaziah's sister managed to hide away Joash, the king's infant son, and six years later Jehoiada the priest made an end of Athaliah and crowned the boy-king, at the same time destroying the temple of Baal at Jerusalem (11. 2–4–18). Before this, there had been a fierce and bloody revolution in Israel, headed by Jehu the son of Nimshi, at the instigation of the prophet Elisha (chs 9 and 10).

There were also perils to Israel's social life; perils that according to one of the two narratives of Saul's accession (1 Sam. 8; see p. 50 above) had been foreseen when it was first proposed that Israel should have a king 'like one of the nations'. These perils had now become actual; the old agricultural economy, based on home-produced foods and barter, had been replaced by a money-economy which brought an increase of wealth, and great landed estates, and poverty to the peasant population.

THE PROPHETS

It was in this new civilized Israel that a series of great prophets arose—Elijah in Ahab's reign, his lesser disciple Elisha, and in the next century Amos and Hosea in the northern kingdom and Isaiah and Micah in Judah, who warned Israel with increasing definiteness of the imminence of the LORD's judgement on the people's corporate sin—for it is with this common sin that they are primarily concerned, rather than with the personal sins of individuals. They denounce (i) the false and unreal worship of the LORD; (ii) the forsaking of him to go after 'other gods'; (iii) the oppression of the poor. Also (iv) they have to interpret the external threat of defeat by the irresistible military power of Assyria, and to prepare the people for much suffering. We will take these headings in order.

But first it needs to be said that it is impossible to exaggerate the greatness of these prophets and their successors, and the debt which our religion owes to them. Their stature is such that a generation ago it was commonly said that they were the creators of Israel's faith; as if the religion of Israel before they appeared had been no different from that of the neighbouring nations. Certainly in the working out of the LORD's purpose they were his most notable instruments. But it is simply not true to say that they brought to Israel a faith unknown before; they are recalling Israel to a faith which has been forgotten. They themselves stand within the Covenant, and they continually appeal to the deliverance from Egypt in the Exodus as the basic fact of Israel's existence. See for instance Amos 2. 9–10, 3. 1, 9. 7; Hosea 2. 15, 11. 1, 12. 13, 13. 4.

(i) *The Unreal Worship of the LORD*

Amos is the earliest of the writing prophets, and his style is so plain, simple and powerful, that it is easy for everyone to understand. He was a herdsman from Tekoa in Judah; he tells in 7. 14–15 how the LORD had called him to go and prophesy in Israel, at the royal sanctuary of Bethel (vv. 10–13). It was in Jeroboam II's reign, some time before or after 760 B.C. That which he condemns is a superficial nationalistic religion, which takes for granted that because the Lord is their national God, therefore he will always take their side and treat them as his favourites.

As a countryman, he gives some splendid pictures of the glory of God in nature (4. 13; 5. 8; 9. 6). But his primary concern is with man's responsibility before God. He begins his prophecies with some stanzas declaring the judgement of the Lord on the surrounding peoples: the cities of Damascus, Gaza, Tyre, the tribes of Edom, Ammon, Moab; then comes the turn of Judah, and finally of Israel (1. 2–2. 16). Above all, there is the sin of unreal worship; see 4. 4–5; 5. 4–8, 14. In 5. 16–20 we gather that the people are hopefully anticipating a 'Day of the Lord', when God will come to bless them and bring them joy, security, and peace. Amos says that the Day will be the very reverse of what they think. The Day will be darkness and not light; he hates, he despises their feasts, he will not have their sacrifices (5. 18, 22–23), so long as they think they can sin as they please, and then offer gifts to buy his favour. He has sent one warning after another, and they have not repented (4. 6–13).

Isaiah gives a similar message to Jerusalem, in chs. 1 and 2. 5–22; *Micah* in 6. 1–8. Perhaps the clearest statement of the principle is in *Jeremiah* ch. 7, where the prophet cries Woe on the people who put their trust in the Temple (7. 4). If they amend their lives and forsake their injustice in the law-courts, their cruelty to the helpless, and their worship of strange gods, all will be well (7. 5–7). But they think they can 'steal, murder, and commit adultery, and swear falsely, and burn incense to Baal, and walk after other gods' *and then* come and stand before the Lord in his house, and say 'We are delivered', that they may do all these abominations (7. 9–10). That is to make God's Temple into a 'den of robbers' (7. 11). These last words were quoted by our Lord when he cleansed the Temple (Mark 11. 17); he meant (as Jeremiah meant) that the Temple was being used like a cave which a bandit has among the mountains, where he retires for safety from pursuit after committing his robberies: or as we might say, like using gifts to religious causes as a sort of celestial insurance policy against the more unpleasant consequences of wrongdoing. The prophets say that the Lord God will not have it. He is the living God, and his relation to his people is

a personal relation. It is an insult to him, therefore, when people
come to offer him sacrifices and make their prayers, as those who are
buying his favour, in order to make things safe for themselves. The
first lesson that man must learn about his relation to God is that he
must fear him, and treat as holy his holy Name, instead of profaning
it by formalism and religious falsehood. 'Hallowed be thy Name.'

(ii) *The Worship of Other Gods*

Hosea's style, unfortunately, is as abrupt, jerky, and disconnected
as that of Amos is coherent and plain. The first three chapters, however, in which he tells us his life-story are mostly clear enough.

It is a story of an unhappy marriage. It is probably right to take
Hosea 1. 2, where the prophet is told by the LORD to marry an
adulterous woman, as describing what the marriage afterwards
turned out to be. Hosea was at first happily married to Gomer, and
she afterwards proved unfaithful and committed adultery; perhaps
the second and third children were thus born. From this sad experience of his own broken marriage Hosea learnt that the LORD loved
Israel: He was Israel's true husband, and Israel his Bride; and Israel
had been unfaithful to him, and had committed adultery against
him, in going after the nature-gods of Canaan. Hosea speaks in
several places as if Israel had truly loved him when he espoused her
and made the Covenant with her in the days of Moses, and describes her future return to him, after her period of chastisement, as
a renewal of her first love:

And she shall make answer there,
　As in the days of her youth,
　And as in the day when she came up out of the land of Egypt (2. 15).

Clearly Gomer had at one time truly loved Hosea.

Hosea, in grief over his ruined home, sent his wife away; after
some years it seems that he found her serving as a slave, for he tells
us that he brought her back (3. 1, 2), and kept her for a time deprived
of conjugal rights. For he loved his wife, and his human love and
sorrow taught him to apply these terms to God. 'When Israel was
a child, then I loved him, and called my son out of Egypt' (11. 1).
But Israel has gone after her 'other lovers', and has forsaken him,

though it was really he and not the Baalim who had given her the corn and the wine and the oil (2. 8). Therefore he must deal severely with her, and deprive her of the gifts of civilization (2. 9–14), till she returns at last to her true husband (2. 7–8), with a renewal of her love (2. 15).

Here, then, we have the beginning of a theme which runs through the two Testaments. Hosea sees Israel as the LORD's unfaithful Bride, who must be punished for her unchastity; and this theme is taken up by Jeremiah (2. 1–3; 3. 1–13 etc.) and Ezekiel (ch. 16). We shall see how the prophets of the Exile witness the execution of this sentence; and then, when Israel in exile has begun to learn repentance, there come the promises of the Messianic days when she shall be the faithful wife (Isa. 54. 1–8; 62. 4–5) and Mother (Isa. 66. 10–13). Our Lord, when he comes, is the Bridegroom (the King's Son in the parable of the Wedding-Feast, Matt. 22. 2, and the Bridegroom in that of the Ten Virgins, Matt. 25. 1–13); and St. Paul works out at length the analogy of Christ the Bridegroom and Israel (the Church) as his Bride in Eph. 5. 22–23.

(iii) *Social Iniquity*

Almost all the prophets speak of the sin of oppression of the poor. Large landowners get the peasant into their power. There is sharp practice in buying farm produce, in selling debtors into slavery, in unjust judgements in the law-courts, in the eviction of farmers from their lands.

Some instances are:

Amos 5. 11–12: 'Forasmuch as ye trample on the poor, and take exactions from him of wheat' . . . 'Ye that afflict the just, that take a bribe, and that turn aside the needy in the gate (the law-court) from their right. . . .'

6. 3–6: They 'that lie upon beds of ivory, and stretch themselves upon their couches, and eat the lambs out of the flocks, and the calves out of the midst of the stall; that sing idle songs to the sound of the viol; that devise for themselves instruments of music, like David; that drink wine out of bowls, and anoint themselves with the chief ointments: but they are not grieved for the affliction of Joseph. . . .'

8. 5–6: '... making the ephah small, and the shekel great, and dealing falsely with balances of deceit; that we may buy the poor for silver, and the needy for a pair of shoes, and sell the refuse of the wheat.'

Isaiah 3. 14–15: 'The LORD will enter into judgement with the elders of his people and the princes thereof. It is ye that have eaten up the vine-yard; the spoil of the poor is in your houses. What mean ye that ye crush My people, and grind the faces of the poor? saith the Lord, the LORD of Hosts.'

5. 8–10: 'Woe unto them that join house to house, and field to field, till there be no room, and ye be made to dwell alone in the midst of the land! In mine ears saith the LORD of Hosts, Of a truth many houses shall be desolate, even great and fair, without inhabitant'—and the rest of ch. 5.

Micah 2. 2: 'They covet fields, and seize them, and houses, and take them away; and they oppress a man and his house, even a man and his heritage.'

Yet none of the prophets can be called 'labour leaders' or 'champions of the working class'. They care about Israel as a whole, because Israel is the people of the LORD. They stand up for the poor because they form part of his Israel, and they denounce the sins of the rich and powerful because these are specially flagrant. They do not stand up for the rights of man in Rousseau's sense, but because man is precious in God's sight.

(iv) The Peril from Assyria

In the days of Amos and Hosea the peril of Assyrian militarism had begun to be serious; these prophets foresaw and foretold defeat and deportation. In the days of Isaiah the peril had come very near. The people of Judah witnessed the destruction of the sister-kingdom, and throughout Isaiah's lifetime the 'war of nerves' was going on. The politicians of these small nations saw a choice between a policy of 'appeasement' towards the Assyrian king, involving the payment of a heavy tribute (2 Kings 15. 19–20, 18. 13–16), with the threat of eventual deportation (cf. 2 Kings 18. 31–32), and a policy of seeking alliances, especially with Egypt (cf. Isa. 30. 1–5; 31. 1–3).

Isaiah in his later years became the foremost citizen of Jerusalem, and took a great part in politics. Yet he never became a partisan of either of the rival policies, but faced the issues in a serene faith in God as the Lord of history. When he was still young, he denounced King Ahaz and his policy of appeasement (Isa. 7. 1–17). What manner of man Ahaz was may be gathered from 2 Kings 16; he called in the help of the Assyrian king against the kingdoms of Syria and Israel, and after he had destroyed Damascus Ahaz went to meet him there, and ordered an Assyrian altar to be built in the temple at Jerusalem, to offer sacrifices to the Assyrian god Asshur, as being evidently the strongest of all the gods (2 Kings 16. 10–16); in order to placate the LORD, he offered up his eldest son in sacrifice, as the costliest offering that he could make (16. 3).

It was no longer, as in the days of Hosea, a matter of standing up against the worship of the nature-gods of Canaan. Now, in terror of their lives, men were seeking the help of any gods in heaven or hell that might save them from disaster. It was in the midst of all this that Isaiah held to his faith in the LORD as the Lord of history. He saw the dreaded master of the irresistible military machine as an instrument in the LORD's hand, sent by him to chastise his own sinful people (Isa. 10. 5–15); yet no more able to do anything without God's over-ruling control than an axe or a staff is able to assert itself against him who wields it (verse 15):

'Ho, Assyrian, the rod of mine anger,
The staff in whose hand is mine indignation!
I will send him against a profane nation,
And against the people of my wrath will I give him a charge,
　　To take the spoil,
　　And to take the prey,
And to tread them down like the mire of the streets.
　　Howbeit he meaneth not so,
　　Neither doth his heart think so;
　　But it is in his heart to destroy,
　　And to cut off nations not a few.' (10. 5–7.)

He boasts of his field-marshals: 'Are not my princes all of them kings?'—and of the cities which he has sacked. But the last word lies with God:

'Wherefore it shall come to pass, that when the LORD hath performed
his whole work upon mount Zion and on Jerusalem,
    I will punish the fruit of the stout heart of the king of Assyria,
    And the glory of his high looks.
For he hath said, "By the strength of my hand I have done it,
    And by my wisdom; for I am prudent: . . .
    And my hand hath found as a nest the riches of the peoples;
    And as one gathereth eggs that are forsaken,
    Have I gathered all the earth:
    And there was none that moved the wing,
    Or that opened the mouth, or chirped."
Shall the axe boast itself against him that heweth therewith?
Shall the saw magnify itself against him that shaketh it?
As if a rod should shake them that lift it up,
Or as if a staff should lift up him that is not wood.' (10. 12–15.)

As Isaiah was sure that after the LORD had 'performed his whole
work upon mount Zion and upon Jerusalem', his judgement would
fall upon Assyria (10. 12), so he believed that his chastisement of
Jerusalem would lead to salvation, through the survival of a
faithful Remnant.

'It shall come to pass that he that is left in Zion,
And he that remaineth in Jerusalem,
    Shall be called holy,
Even every one that is written among the living at Jerusalem:
When the LORD shall have washed away the filth of the daughters of Zion,
And shall have purged the blood of Jerusalem from the midst thereof,
    By the spirit of judgment,
    And by the spirit of burning.' (4. 3–4.)

The tree would have to be cut down, without mercy; yet the
stump would remain (6. 13); and from the stump a new living shoot
would spring up:

There shall come forth a shoot out of the stock of Jesse,
And a branch out of his roots shall bear fruit (11. 1; p. 58 above).

'A remnant shall return' (*Shear-yashub*). He gave that name to his
son (7. 3), in order to proclaim to all the doctrine of the Remnant.

The faithful Remnant, purified through suffering, would no longer follow a policy of appeasement, but would put its trust in the Holy One of Israel (10. 20–21). A nucleus of that Remnant was already discernible in the band of disciples which he gathered round him, disciples whom he believed God had given him, that through them he might work out his gracious purpose:

> Behold, I and the children whom God hath given me
> Are for signs and wonders in Israel,
> From the LORD of Hosts, which dwelleth in Mount Zion (8. 18).

The conception of a faithful Remnant had already appeared in the story of Elijah, who was told that he was not alone, as he thought, in his witness to the LORD and his truth (1 Kings 19. 10, 14):

> I have been very jealous for the LORD, the God of Hosts; for the children of Israel have forsaken thy covenant, thrown down thine altars, and slain thy prophets with the sword: and I, even I only, am left, and they seek my life, to take it away;

but there were seven thousand in Israel who had not bowed the knee to Baal (verse 18).

When at last Jerusalem was destroyed, there was a faithful Remnant which passed through the waters of judgement, and in which God's Purpose of salvation was carried on. Always after that there was a faithful Remnant, of those who were Israelites indeed. The idea, though not the name, comes again in the Son of Man prophecy of Daniel ch. 7 (see p. 117 below). When the Son of God hung on the Cross, the faithful Remnant existed in his person. St. Paul speaks of the Christians who believed in the Messiah though Israel as a whole had rejected him, as 'a Remnant according to the election of grace' (Rom. 11. 5) like the seven thousand who were found faithful in the time of Elijah (verses 2–4).

God's salvation always brings with it judgement. But in the midst of judgement there is always the Remnant, through which God's universal Purpose goes forward.

DEUTERONOMY AND JOSIAH'S REFORM

The prophets speak to a large extent (if the phrase may be allowed) in negative terms, convicting Israel of sin, throwing on contemporary life the light of God's truth which shows up the evil there. But there is another book, edited about the same time, which sets out positively and constructively the pattern of what Israel's life should be; this is the Book of Deuteronomy, which according to the generally accepted view is that Book of the Law which was found in the Temple by Hilkiah, as is related in 2 Kings 22. 8, and was put into practice in the Covenant made by King Josiah (23. 1–24). The date of this was 621 B.C. In spite of certain difficulties which remain only partly solved, this identification holds the field, and we can confidently say that the Book that Josiah had in his hands consisted of at least Deut. 12–26, though (as seems certain) additions were being made to the book for twenty or more years after.

In Deuteronomy the three main subjects of the prophetic preaching reappear somewhat as follows:

(i) The prophets had condemned the unreal worship of the LORD God. In Deuteronomy we get, in chapters 4–11, splendid homilies about the faith of Israel, resting on the LORD's own act and the initiative which he took in redeeming Israel out of Egypt, not because of any merits on Israel's part, but solely because of his love (7. 7–8). We get the great *Shema'*:

'Hear, O Israel, the LORD our God is one LORD; and thou shalt love the LORD thy God with all thy heart and with all thy soul and with all thy strength. And these words which I command thee this day shall be upon thine heart; and thou shalt teach them diligently unto thy children. . . .' (6. 4–7.)

On Israel's loyalty to this faith and the spiritual service of the LORD which it demands, all its well-being and prosperity depends; disloyalty will as certainly bring judgement and punishment. Israel must remember God's dealing with it in the past: 'remember, remember . . .' (5. 15; 7. 18; 8. 2, 18; 9. 7, 27 etc.).

(ii) The formal worship of the LORD, with dignity and splendour, was provided for by the centralization of all sacrifice in the great Temple at Jerusalem, and the destruction of all the country shrines which had originally been dedicated to Baal. This was ordered in Deut. 12. 1–7, 13–14, and carried out by Josiah (2 Kings 23. 4–15); it was however not a wholly new thing, for Hezekiah, one hundred years before, had done something along these lines (2 Kings 18. 4). The intention was to cut off at the root the whole of the Canaanite nature-religion, that henceforth the religion of Israel might be kept pure from pagan contamination. The great agricultural festivals, which had originally been Baal-festivals, were now celebrated at Jerusalem in honour of the LORD, as is ordered in chapter 16. There was the Passover, the memorial of the deliverance from Egypt (16. 1–2), with the agricultural feast of Unleavened Bread (16. 3–4); then the Feast of Weeks, at the completion of the wheat-harvest (16. 9–12); and the great annual festival in the autumn (16. 13–16).

It was true indeed that, just as no formal covenant or ordinance could guard against the unreal worship of the LORD God, so no prohibition of pagan practices could wholly stamp them out; and we find in Jer. 44. 17–19, 25, that incense was still being burned to the Queen of Heaven (Astarte) forty years later, after the Fall of Jerusalem: it had stopped in 621 B.C., and then had started again (44. 18). Yet it was a great thing indeed that the repudiation of idolatrous worship was now embodied in a covenant, solemnly entered on by king and people, and preserved in permanent form in a written book (2 Kings 23. 2–3). Indeed, this Book of Deuteronomy had now been accepted by Israel as authoritative and binding; in other words, it had become Scripture.

We are so used to having a Bible that it is easy to forget that there was once a time when no Bible existed, and, more than that, when the idea which the word 'Bible' signifies had not been thought of. There were of course in 621 B.C. many writings in existence which are now part of the Bible, but they were not solemnly authorized or treated as 'canonical'. But when Deuteronomy was accepted by king and people as the Book of the Covenant, the Book that con-

tained God's commandments and that expressed Israel's faith, Israel
had begun to have a Bible.

(iii) The prophets had denounced social unrighteousness. Deuteronomy shows throughout how deep an impression their teaching
had made. The regulations in chapters 12–26 are like a blue-print of
the national life; the king is told what his duty is, and that he is to
read in the book of the Law every day, 'that his heart be not lifted
up above his breathren' (17. 14–20); judges must not pervert justice,
nor take bribes (16. 18–20). There is a multitude of detailed regulations, largely taken from earlier codes, in chapters 19–26. But there
is also an inculcation of generosity and kindliness, going beyond the
written rule, as in 15. 7–11; 22. 1–3 (lost property); 23. 19, 24. 10–13
(loans). The Book represents a determined effort to see the whole
national life as under the rule of the LORD, and the making of
Josiah's Covenant was the nation's acknowledgement of him as its
King.

The prophet Jeremiah seems to have taken his part in supporting
the Reform in 621; 11. 1–8 must surely belong to this date. But as
time went on, he became deeply dissatisfied with the results of the
Reform. We read in chapter 26 of a great Sermon which he preached
in the Temple, and which almost cost him his life; this was early
in the reign of Jehoiakim, in 609 or 608. The text of the Sermon is
given in chapter 7 (see p. 63 above); people were taking pride in
their temple (7. 4), and trusting that all would be well. But Jeremiah
saw that all was not well:

'The heart is deceitful above all things, and it is desperately sick; who
can know it? I the LORD search the heart, I try the reins, even to give to
every man according to his ways, according to the fruit of his doings.'
(17. 9–10.)

He could only expect that the worst would happen.

Yet even so, the Reform had not been in vain. The great
Covenant had been made; the people had bound themselves to the
old Mosaic faith; the Baal-shrines had disappeared; the principle of
one God, one Temple, one place of sacrifice, had been accepted; it
had been affirmed that the whole life of the nation was under the

LORD's rule; and they now had his written Law, authoritative and formally canonized.

A supreme trial now lay before them, the coming destruction of city and temple, and the extinction of the nation as a political unit. It did count for a great deal that before that hour of Israel's passion a flag had been hoisted, and nailed to the mast. The duty that lay before them was to keep that flag flying. In spite of many faults and failures, they did keep that flag flying; and it is flying still today wherever the Church confesses its faith. The Reformation under Josiah was not in vain.

CHAPTER VII

'Chastened and not killed'

JEREMIAH, EZEKIEL : ISAIAH 2

Dates

Death of Josiah; Jehoiakim king	609
Jehoiachin (Coniah), king	598
First Deportation; Zedekiah king	598
Fall of Jerusalem and Second Deportation	587

Jeremiah's ministry, 626 till after 587
Ezekiel deported, 598; ministry, 594–572
Second Isaiah's ministry, before 538 and probably also after that date.

THE northern kingdom had perished in 721 B.C. The southern kingdom lasted for 135 years longer, when it too perished with the Fall of Jerusalem in 587 B.C. We cannot exaggerate the completeness of the disaster, when the whole fabric of the political, economic, and social life of the nation was destroyed, all the local traditions brought to an end, the city sacked, the Temple burnt with fire, the people (all but a few, mostly of the lowest class) deported to Mesopotamia. The intention of the conquerors was that the distinctive life of the free peoples should disappear, so that they might give no trouble and it might be possible to rule them. Assyria began and Babylon continued the practice of wholesale deportations.

For defeated Judah, the extinction of the nation as a political unit was the cruellest possible trial. Jeremiah and Ezekiel were the two prophets who brought them through it, telling them that the LORD was in control of all that happened, and was chastizing them for their sins; therefore they must accept it all as from him, believing in him and trusting him, and confessing their sin.

WAYS OF EVASION

There were two ways of evading their duty. The first amounted to apostasy from their faith; it was to say that the LORD the God of Israel had been overpowered by the stronger gods of Babylon.

This argument had been put to their great-grandfathers a hundred years before, by Sennacherib's Rabshakeh (Field Marshal) in 701. It was to say that all the nations had their gods, and none of these gods had been able to deliver their people; all in turn had been over-whelmed. 'Where are the gods of Hamath and Arpad? of Sephar-vaim, of Hena and Ivvah?' The LORD had been unable to save Samaria; it was vain to think that Jerusalem would escape (2 Kings 18. 33–36).

It would seem that such people as the Moabites, who wor-shipped their god Chemosh, could have no answer to such an argu-ment; the logic of the facts would be conclusive proof that the gods of Babylon were stronger than their own little tribal god. And the LORD was the tribal God of Israel. But he was different. And so in chapter 19 we are told how king Hezekiah saw the matter. He prays to the LORD, confesses him to be God over all nations and kingdoms, being the creator of heaven and earth; says that of course the nations have been destroyed and their gods thrown into the fire, 'for they were no gods, but the work of men's hands, wood and stone'; and prays that he will vindicate his honour by delivering Jerusalem (19. 15–19).

On that occasion Jerusalem was delivered; but Hezekiah's faith rested on grounds that would prove to be firm in 587, when the city was *not* delivered. Of course the Israelites were continually tempted, as we are, to allow their faith to drop back on to a pagan level, and think of God as if he existed for the sake of their own well-being and security. But the tradition of the faith forbade that.

For when the blow fell, there was no denying the fact that since the days of Amos, 180 years before, a succession of prophets had said that he would chastise his People in just this way because of their sin. These prophecies had been most terribly verified by the event. There was, then, nothing for them to do but accept the fact, and confess that they had sinned. When they had done this difficult thing, the next point that became clear was that, if the LORD had been chastising them, that proved that he cared about them, and had a purpose for them which he had yet to complete. He who had smitten was able to save. Thus it came about that in the time of the

Exile a series of 'Messianic' prophecies appeared, of a fulness and richness hitherto unknown.

There was a second way of evading the issue, by a superficial optimism. Many were beguiled by this in the years following the First Deportation in 598, when King Jehoiachin surrendered, and the Babylonians removed from the temple most of what was of value, and took away 10,000 captives, king and nobles and fighting men and artisans (2 Kings 24. 10–17). Among these was the young priest Ezekiel (Ezek. 1. 2). The difference between those who went and those who stayed seemed to Jeremiah like the difference between 'good figs, and figs that could not be eaten, they were so bad' (Jer. 24).

The temptation now was to say, 'It is going to be all right. The LORD delivered his people before in the time of King Hezekiah, and he will do so again. Within two years the exiles will be back home again, with the vessels belonging to the temple; thus saith the LORD.' Exactly this was said by the prophet Hananiah, in the LORD's name (Jer. 28. 1–4); and he took a wooden yoke which Jeremiah was wearing over his shoulders, as a token of the servitude which the LORD was imposing on Judah and the surrounding nations (cf. 27. 2), and broke the yoke before the people, saying, 'Thus saith the LORD, Even so will I break the yoke of Nebuchadnezzar King of Babylon' (28. 5–11). Hananiah had won the first round. Jeremiah, however, tells us that the word of the LORD came to him that he must replace the wooden yoke with a yoke of iron, and explain what this meant, and say to Hananiah that he was making the people to trust in a lie, and would die within the year because he had spoken rebellion against the LORD; and that Hananiah died in the seventh month (28. 12–17).

THE PROPHETIC WORD

Ezekiel was saying much the same to the exiles in Babylon. They must not listen to the plausible prophets 'who seduce my people, saying Peace, where there is no peace' (13. 1–10). Those prophets are building a wall with untempered mortar, and the wall is going to come crashing down (13. 10–16). Jerusalem is going to fall; it must fall, because of the sins of the people (see chapter 8, where the prophet is taken in a trance to Jerusalem, and sees the abominations being practised there; chapters 9, 10 and 11 continue with a 'mystical' description of the fall of the city). He uses one parable after another to bring home to the exiles that it will be so and must be so; they themselves must confess their sin (chapter 18), and the sin of rebellion against the LORD which has been shown in each period of the nation's history from the beginning (20. 1–44).

The prophet's word was indeed to be vindicated by the event; but the cost of it to Ezekiel himself can be guessed from what he tells us of his own wife's death. He was told by the LORD that he was to make no sign of mourning, though his heart was breaking with grief:

'The word of the LORD came unto me, saying,
> "Son of man, behold, I take away from thee the desire of thine eyes
> > with a stroke:
> Yet neither shalt thou mourn nor weep,
> Neither let thy tears run down.
> Sigh, but not aloud;
> Make no mourning for the dead . . ."

So I spake unto the people in the morning; and at even my wife died: and I did in the morning as I was commanded' (24. 15–18).

When the people asked what could be the reason for this extraordinary behaviour, he told them that it would be so with them when the City fell; it would be so utterly crushing a blow that it would leave them speechless, and unable even to weep:

'Thus saith the Lord GOD:
> Behold, I will profane my sanctuary,
> > The pride of your power,
> > The desire of your eyes,
> > And that which your soul pitieth:
> > And your sons and your daughters whom ye have left behind
> > > shall fall by the sword.
> And ye shall do as I have done: . . .
> > Ye shall not mourn nor weep;
> > But ye shall pine away in your iniquities,
> > And moan one toward another.

Thus shall Ezekiel be to you a sign;
According to all that he hath done shall ye do:
When this cometh, then shall ye know that I am the Lord GOD'
(24. 21–4).

In Ezek. 37 we have the vision of the Valley of the Dry Bones:
the valley was like the site of a battlefield. Could those bones live?
He was told to prophesy, and bid Spirit, wind, breath (these are all
one word in Hebrew) to enter into those slain that they might live.
He prophesied, and there was a weird movement of bones coming
together, and flesh and sinews covering the bones, so that they
had the semblance of real men; but there was no life in them (37.
1–8). Such, Ezekiel thought, were the Israelites to whom he prophesied. They had at the catastrophe been a mob of survivors, a social
structure completely broken up into isolated individuals. As he
prophesied, they seemed to be coming together into something
which bore some remote likeness to what the People of God should
be: but there was no life there, they were quite dead. They were
saying, 'Our bones are dried up, out hope is lost, we are clean cut
off' (37. 11). But he is told that he must go on prophesying, till at
last they 'stand on their feet, an exceeding great army'.

Meanwhile Jeremiah had written to the exiles of the First Deportation a famous letter (Jer. 29. 1–3) in which he told them to settle
down in Babylonia, build houses, and seek the peace of the city
whither they were carried away captive; for there would be no
speedy return; it would not be for seventy years (4–10). But the
LORD had the whole matter in hand (verse 11), and they must pray
to him in Babylon (12): 'and ye shall seek me and find me, when ye
shall seek for me with all your heart' (13). But the immediate
prospect for Jerusalem was ruin (16–19).

Jer. 29. 13, which had just been quoted, is almost word for word
the same as Deut. 4. 29. There it is said (Deut. 4. 25–26) that if the
people sin and corrupt themselves, they shall perish out of the land
of Canaan, and shall be scattered in foreign lands (27), where they
will be subject to the gods of the land who are no-gods (28). But if
from thence they seek the LORD their God, they shall find him, if
they seek with all their heart and all their soul (29) for he will not

fail them (30, 31). For the revelation of the LORD in his mighty works wrought out in history is absolutely unique, and there is nothing like it among all the religions of the nations (32–35). For 'the LORD, he is God, in heaven above and earth beneath; there is none else' (verse 39).

When the city fell, it was an utterly crushing blow. Their Temple had been desecrated and burnt with fire, the city walls demolished, and the houses reduced to ruins; most of their sons and daughters had suffered violent death or things worse than death, or had died of starvation. (All this is pictured in Lamentations 2. 15–22). It was the hour of Israel's passion. But now out of the midst of suffering came hope; a hope based on a faith that faced all the facts and claimed no exemption: faith that the LORD the God of Israel was the Lord of the whole earth and the ruler of history; faith that in his dealings with Israel he had been righteous; and a hope that looked towards the future accomplishment of his purpose in history.

ISRAEL IN EXILE

We have no historical narrative of this period. But we can infer a great deal from the facts which we know:

(1) The faithful Israelites did not become absorbed in the Mesopotamian proletariat, but held together as a believing and worshipping community. In Ezekiel's day, as we have seen, they were at least holding together. A generation later, Second Isaiah could address to them glowing words of encouragement, and before the end of the century a strong band of exiles had returned to Jerusalem, and had succeeded in rebuilding the Temple. It follows from this that the exiles had found means to meet together and worship God and be instructed in the Faith, and grow together into a believing community.

(2) The writings containing their old traditions were preserved by these Jews of the Exile: most of Genesis, some of Exodus and Numbers, Deuteronomy; the books from Joshua to Kings in an unfinished state, the books of the pre-exilic prophets, and a number of psalms. They preserved these writings not for antiquarian pur-

poses, but because their whole faith rested on the LORD's action in history, and these were the records of his dealings with Abraham, Isaac, and Jacob, and above all of the Deliverance from Egypt and the Covenant; and after that, of the story of their life in Canaan and the sin against the LORD for which they were now suffering the punishment of exile. Every Israelite needed to know these things: therefore he needed to be told, indeed to be systematically instructed in what his membership in Israel involved, as a faith to believe and a duty to do.

(3) In present-day Judaism there exists the Synagogue, and its primary purpose is what was said in the last sentence: to instruct and exercise the Jew in his faith and duty. In New Testament days multitudes of Synagogues were to be found, wherever there were Jews. How early they began, we do not know. But there is a description in Neh. 8 of an open-air meeting, perhaps about 428 B.C., which recalls several features of the Synagogue: Ezra reads from the Book of the Law, standing in a pulpit of wood (8. 1–4); the people stand up and answer 'Amen' (6); the Levites explain the meaning of what has been read (7–8).

In the old days in Canaan, the people continually met at various sanctuaries, and at the Temple. But neither there, nor anywhere else in antiquity, were buildings constructed to house a congregation. An ancient sanctuary was built to house the image of the god, or (in the case of Solomon's temple) the sacred Ark, and provide strong-rooms for the offerings; the people were never allowed inside, but stood round the altar in the open air. In Babylonia there was nowhere for them to meet, except in some house; and we hear of them meeting in Ezekiel's house (Ezek. 8. 1; 14. 1; 20. 1). For serious religious instruction a house was necessary; and whenever it was that such houses began to be specially built, then for the first time in history buildings were being built to hold a congregation. The inference seems certain, that the first beginnings of the Synagogue took place early in the Exile.

The Christian reader may reflect that our churches are still synagogues, with pulpit, a lectern, and benches; but containing also a font for the baptismal water, and a table for the Lord's Supper.

Further, the items of the synagogue service—prayer and praise, scripture readings and exposition of scripture—reappear in our ante-communion service, and again in Mattins or Evensong with sermon; while the action at the Lord's Table which begins with the Offertory and goes on to the Consecration and Communion, is the liturgical action which has taken the place of the sacrifices offered in the Temple.

ISAIAH OF BABYLON

We now come to the great prophet and poet and theologian who gave us Isaiah 40–55, chapters which to us are among the most familiar and the most loved in the Old Testament.

But in studying them we make a mistake if we think only of the prophet and forget the believing and worshipping community within which he had grown up and for which he wrote. The date is, as we will see, not long before 538 when Babylon fell to Cyrus the Persian; that is, about 50 years since Ezekiel had begun to preach. We have seen on p. 79 what Ezekiel thought of the exiles at the time when he began his ministry to them; but his work had had its effect, and it is clear that 'Isaiah' is writing for a community which will understand his message and respond to it. It is true that he is not satisfied with them:

> 'Who is blind, but my servant?
> Or deaf, as my messenger that I send?
> Who is blind as he that is at peace with me,
> And blind, as the LORD's servant?' (42. 19).

Yet even so, he can call on them to make the journey to Jerusalem and rebuild the Temple (44. 28). We are at the eve of the Return from Exile.

40. 1–11 is a message to desolate Jerusalem, that her tribulation is over; the LORD is preparing to lead his people back across the desert, to show his power and reign, to gather together his flock (v. 11). The same note is struck in 52. 1–12, of the LORD's approaching work of deliverance; and here in verse 7 we have the word Gospel (*besorah*), which originally denoted the proclamation in a city of

Good Tidings of victory in battle—it is never used for news of defeat—and here the proclamation is that the LORD is ascending his throne that he may reign:

> 'How beautiful upon the mountains
> Are the feet of him that bringeth good tidings,
>> That publisheth peace,
>> That bringeth good tidings of good,
>> That publisheth salvation,
> That saith unto Zion, Thy God reigneth' (52.7).

The God who reigns is the Creator, the God of all the earth, 40. 12–31; he is the First and the Last, 41. 4, 44. 6; the Redeemer, the Saviour, 43. 1, 3. He has indeed inflicted his dreadful judgements on Israel:

> 'Who gave Jacob for a spoil, and Israel to the robbers? Did not the LORD? He against whom we have sinned, and in whose ways they would not walk, neither were they obedient to his law. Therefore he poured out upon him the fury of his anger and the strength of battle, and it set him on fire round about; yet he knew not; and it burned him, yet he laid it not to heart.' (42. 24–25.)

But now the LORD is raising up Cyrus as the instrument of deliverance (44. 28–45. 4). He who is the Lord of History proclaims his purpose through his prophets. But from the pagan gods there is no word; they are dumb, there is no message from them. He challenges the pagan gods:

> 'Produce your cause, saith the LORD;
> Bring forth your strong reasons, saith the King of Jacob.
> Declare the things that are to come hereafter,
>> That we may know that ye are gods;
> Yea, do good, or do evil,
>> That we may be dismayed and behold it together.
> Behold, ye are of nothing, and your work of nought;
> An abomination is he that chooseth you.' (41. 21, 23–4.)

On the pagan gods, Isaiah pours out his scorn; they are no-gods, they are vanity. In 44. 9–20 he has a most satirical passage describing the manufacture of an idol-image; in 46. 1–2 Bel and Nebo, the gods of Babylon, are pictured as being carried into captivity on the backs of weary beasts, when the city falls.

But the LORD, the living and true God, the Creator, is such that his Name must at last become known to all mankind:

'Look unto me, and be ye saved,
    All the ends of the earth:
For I am God, and there is none else.
By myself have I sworn—
    The word is gone forth from my mouth in righteousness, and shall not
        return—
That unto me every knee shall bow,
    Every tongue shall swear.' (45. 22–23.)

And Israel, his servant (49. 3), is in spite of his weakness and failure to be his witness and a light to the Gentiles (49. 6); for

        'I will pour water on the thirsty land,
        And floods upon the dry ground;
        I will pour my Spirit upon thy seed,
        And my blessing upon thine offspring.' (44. 3.)

But we must reserve the four poems about the LORD's Servant till the last section of the next chapter.

CHAPTER VIII

'Behold, thy King cometh unto thee'

THE MESSIANIC PROPHECIES

WE were thinking in the last chapter of Israel in exile, trying to reckon it all up and see what it meant: the desolating catastrophe, the loss of everything in the world that they had held dear, and their present wretched life in an alien land. Yet a message had been coming through that there was a meaning in it. There had been a letter and some prophecies from Jeremiah in far-away Palestine; and with them in Babylonia there had been a hard-faced man, given to queer ecstasies and strange actions, who yet had a wonderful tenderness in him and spoke with such conviction that they could not help but listen:

And as for thee, son of man, the children of thy people talk of thee by the walls and in the doors of the houses, and speak one to another, every one to his brother, saying, "Come, I pray you, and hear the word that cometh forth from the Lord."

And they come unto thee as the people cometh,

And they sit before thee as my people,

And they hear thy words,

　But do them not:

For with their mouth they show much love,

But their heart goeth after their gain.

And lo, thou art unto them as a very lovely song of one that hath a pleasant voice,

　And can play well on an instrument:

For they hear thy words,

　But do them not.

And when *this* cometh to pass (behold, it cometh) then shall they know that a prophet hath been among them (Ezek. 33. 30–3).

Ezekiel refers in the last sentence, no doubt, to the impending news of the final ruin of Jerusalem. It had been a hard, hard message that he had to give. They had sinned against their God, and this terrible calamity had come from him: it was his doing, and he was punishing them for their sin. Yet the message made sense. It was what some of the prophets whom they had dreaded and disliked had been saying for a long time before. But their consciences told them that it was true. And it held within it a spring of wonderful hope; for if it were true, it meant that the LORD, their God, with whom all their previous life had been bound up, was not defeated, had not been overpowered in the disaster that had fallen on Jerusalem, and that he was not indifferent to them now, but still cared for them, and still had a purpose for them.

The message, as it came through and slowly became clear to them, was that he had a great and glorious Purpose in store, wonderful beyond words. He who had in the distant past delivered their fathers from Egypt in the Exodus, would when his time had come deliver them again in *another and a more glorious Exodus*, and lead them back to Jerusalem in triumph; would make with them *a New Covenant*, and reconcile them to himself as a truly converted Israel, *pouring out his Spirit* upon them, that they might truly be his people, and he their God, and forgiving them all their sin. And further, that when *he manifested his glory* in this new deliverance, *all the heathen around them would be brought in*, to share in this new knowledge of him as the gracious and merciful God.

We will now consider these in order; for there is nothing more to be said for the present about the hope of the ideal Davidic King (which is 'the Messianic Hope' in the strict sense of the term) beyond what was said on p. 58, except that a few passages in Jeremiah (esp. 16. 14–15, 23. 5–6) and Ezekiel (34. 23–24, 37. 24–25) show that this Hope was still alive.

THE SECOND EXODUS

Jeremiah, about the time of the catastrophe, was saying that when the LORD's time came there would be a new Deliverance, like the Exodus from Egypt. He says in 23. 7 that then they will no longer invoke the Name of the LORD as of him who brought them up out of Egypt, but of him as the Deliverer who has brought them back from the lands of their exile:

> 'Therefore, behold, the days come, saith the LORD,
> That they shall no more say
>> "As the LORD liveth,
>> Which brought up the children of Israel
>> Out of the land of Egypt";
> But, "As the LORD liveth,
>> Which brought up and which led the seed of the house of Israel
>> Out of the north country,
>>> And from all the countries whither I had driven them":
> And they shall dwell in their own land.' (Jer. 23. 7–8.)

Second Isaiah plainly has this New Exodus in mind, when in 40. 3 he speaks of 'preparing in the wilderness' or desert, 'a highway for our God'; and later on, of the LORD as making 'a way in the sea, and a path in the mighty waters', and bringing forth 'the chariot and the horse' which shall be overthrown, and then says, 'Remember ye not the former things' (the first Exodus) for 'behold I will do a new thing . . . I will even make a way in the wilderness, and rivers in the desert' (43. 16–19); and he refers in verse 20 to the bringing of the water out of the rock in the desert by Moses (Exod. 17. 2–7). This allusion comes again in Isa. 48. 21. The 'drying up of the sea' (Exod. 14) is alluded to again in Isa. 50. 2, 51. 10; and in 52. 12 he says 'Ye shall not go out in haste, neither shall ye go by flight' (as in the first Exodus); 'for the LORD will go before you' (as then in the Pillar of Cloud) 'and the God of Israel will be your rereward.'

THE NEW COVENANT

Of old, the LORD had made his Covenant with Israel at Horeb, after bringing them out of Egypt. Jeremiah sees His future Purpose for Israel as a new Exodus followed by a new Covenant:

> 'Behold, the days come, saith the LORD, that I will make a New Covenant with the house of Israel, and with the house of Judah:
> Not according to the Covenant that I made with their fathers in the day that I took them by the hand to bring them out of the land of Egypt;
> Which my Covenant they brake, althought I was an husband unto them,   Saith the LORD.

But this is the Covenant that I will make with the house of Israel after
    those days, saith the LORD:
  (i) I will put my law in their inward parts,
    And in their heart will I write it;
 (ii)   And I will be their God,
    And they shall be my People;
(iii) And they shall teach no more every man his neighbour,
    And every man his brother,
    Saying, know the LORD:
    For they shall all know me,
    From the least of them unto the greatest of them,
                    Saith the LORD:
 (iv) For I will forgive their iniquity,
    And their sin will I remember no more.' (Jer. 31. 31–34.)

This prophecy is one of the landmarks in the history of the People
of God. The New Covenant is to be characterized (i) by the Law
of God being not a mere external rule, but written in the mind and
will; (ii) Israel will be really and truly the LORD's people; (iii) the
knowledge of God will be no more at second-hand, learnt from some
prophet or priest, but personal knowledge of him; and (iv) there
will be full forgiveness of all their sins.

THE GIFT OF THE SPIRIT

First Isaiah (11.2) had spoken of the six-fold gift of the Spirit
of the LORD to the Messianic king: now we hear of the Spirit to be
poured out on the Messianic people.

The prophecy of Joel, quoted by St. Peter at Pentecost (Acts 2.
17–21), promises that the Spirit of the LORD will be given when the
Day of the LORD comes with cosmic wonders (2. 30–31); the believing Remnant, of whom the first Isaiah had spoken long before,
will receive God's salvation (verse 32); and the sign of the Spirit's
coming will be that all people will receive that same gift that was
given to the prophets: the old shall dream dreams, and the young
shall see visions (verses 28–29). The Spirit is to impart prophetic
insight.

Ezekiel had gone deeper, and had seen the fruit of the Spirit to be a truly converted heart, and a complete and entire obedience to God's will, thus reversing the disobedience and rebelliousness for which he had punished his people in the great catastrophe (Ezek. 36. 25–27):

> 'I will sprinkle clean water upon you
>   And ye shall be clean;
> From all your filthiness, and from all your idols
>   Will I cleanse you.
> A new heart also will I give you,
> And a new spirit will I put within you;
> And I will take away the stony heart out of your flesh,
> And I will give you an heart of flesh.
> And I will put my Spirit within you,
> And cause you to walk in my statutes,
> And ye shall keep my judgments and do them.'

The phrases are different from Jeremiah's prophecy of the New Covenant; but is not the essential meaning as good as identical? The Purpose of the LORD, which began when he called Israel out of Egypt and made the Covenant at Horeb, is to find its fulfilment in the entire acceptance by Israel of its vocation, bringing to God not mere obedience to an outward law, but the love of a wholly surrendered heart. In the centuries that followed, before our LORD's coming, the Israelites were to be set to learn what this meant, and to be tempted to substitute the keeping of an outward law for the loving of God with all their heart and soul and mind. Our Lord, when he came, recalled them to the things that the prophets had said. The Gospel word 'repent' means much more than merely being sorry for past misdeeds; it means literally a 'change of attitude' just such as Ezekiel depicts, in the change from the heart of stone to the heart of flesh, sensitive and responsive.

THE RETURN OF THE PRESENCE

Here we come to a thought closely connected with the New Exodus. When the LORD again takes action to deliver his people, he will be in their midst as at Mount Horeb, where the Covenant was made. The Presence is depicted as having been with them at the Crossing of the Red Sea, in the form of a Pillar of Cloud (Exod. 14. 24); in the wilderness the Pillar 'descended and stood at the door of the Tent' (the Tabernacle), when Moses went in and spoke with him (Exod. 33. 9). The Cloud is mentioned also in Num. 10. 33–36, in connection with the Sacred Ark, which was the other symbol of the LORD's presence with his people.

When the Ark was lost to the Philistines in the days of Eli, the baby that was then born was called *Ichabod*, 'The Glory is departed from Israel' (1 Sam. 4. 21); for this word 'Glory' is constantly found as a description of the Presence on the Ark. When the Ark had been recovered and had been brought into Solomon's temple, we read:

'And it came to pass, when the priests were gone out of the holy place, that the Cloud filled the house of the LORD, so that the priests could not stand to minister by reason of the Cloud; for the Glory of the LORD filled the house of the LORD.' (1 Kings 8. 10, 11.)

When Jerusalem was taken and the Temple burned with fire, Ezekiel tells us how the Presence departed. This came to him in a long trance-like experience (from Ezek. 8. 1 to 10. 25) in which he saw, first the idolatries being carried on in the Temple (chapter 8), then the slaughter at the fall of the city (chapter 9), then the vision of the Presence in the cherub chariot (chapter 10), which at 10. 19 is seen 'at the door of the east gate of the LORD's house' and in 11. 22–23 is seen moving away and resting on the Mount of Olives as It departs.

But It would come back. After Ezekiel has described the plan of the rebuilt city and Temple, he sees the Presence returning and entering the House by the east gate:

'And, behold, the Glory of the God of Israel came from the way of the east and his voice was like the sound of many waters; and the earth shined with his Glory. . . . And the Glory of the LORD came into the house, by the way of the gate whose prospect is toward the east . . . and behold, the Glory of the LORD filled the house. And I heard one speaking unto me out of the house; and a man stood by me. And he said unto me,

"Son of man, this is the place of my throne,

And the place of the soles of my feet,
Where I will dwell in the midst of the children of Israel for ever:
And the house of Israel shall no more defile my holy name." '
   (Ezek. 43. 2, 4–7.)

Ezekiel is permitted to make known to them what is to be the
form of the house, and the ordinances connected with it, provided
that they are truly penitent and are 'ashamed of all that they have
done' (verses 10–11).

We are compelled to say that the prophet was mistaken, as
regards the time. So were other prophets after him, who likewise
believed that the Day of the LORD was near, and some psalmists also.
The hope of the Return of the LORD to fill the Temple with his
Presence was not fulfilled when the exiles returned to Jerusalem and
rebuilt the Temple. We shall see that it, with the other elements
of the Messianic Hope, was fulfilled when Jesus came. But if it
was indeed fulfilled in our Lord, that means that the LORD God
kept his people waiting a long time; we, as we look at the history,
can see that those centuries were for the Israel of God an important
period of discipline.

Were they then sustained through this time of discipline by a
hope which was mistaken? No: for the substance of the hope was
not mistaken; and since the Purpose is God's Purpose, it is bound to
be greater than our limited minds can take in: we are to face the
future in hope, believing in God. Those servants of God in the Old
Testament period looked for an Event which did not come when
and as they expected it. But the God in whom they hoped had not
forgotten his purpose; nor had he forgotten *them*, for we are
assured in the New Testament that the Old Testament saints who
prepared the way for our Lord's Kingdom, do enter into it: they
with us, and we with them (Heb. 11. 39, 40). Similarly our Lord
spoke of Abraham, Isaac, and Jacob as 'in the Kingdom of God'
(Matt. 8. 11; Luke 13. 28).

G

THE HOPE FOR ALL NATIONS

Long before the Exile, the Israelites had realized that the LORD the God of Israel was interested in people of other nations, being indeed the one true God. Naaman the Syrian went to Elisha the prophet of Israel to be healed of his leprosy, and became convinced that 'there is no God in all the earth, but in Israel' (2 Kings 5. 15). Amos believed that the LORD who brought Israel out of Egypt had no less brought the Philistines from Crete and the Syrians from Kir (Amos 9. 7). Isaiah received a request for an oracle from the 'Ethiopians' who lived far away up the river Nile (chapter 18); and his book and those of Jeremiah and Ezekiel contain many prophecies addressed to surrounding nations.

During the Exile it became clear that as the LORD the God of Israel was the creator of all men, so the knowledge of him that Israel had received must come at last to all men. We have already quoted, on p. 84, the great text of Isa. 45. 22–23, that because he is God and there is none else, to him every knee shall bow, every tongue shall swear.

Elsewhere the coming in of the Gentiles is explicitly connected with the future Day when God comes to save his People, and the age of miracles begins again. This connexion is clearly made, for instance in Ps. 102, and in Zech. 2. 10–13. Often it is not clear what part the Gentile nations are to play in that great Day. In Isa. 60 the light is seen shining on Jerusalem, and the Gentiles are seen coming, bringing home the scattered Israelites; they provide transport (verses 4, 9), they offer their gifts (verses 6, 9, 13), they build the walls (verse 10), they bow themselves down before them (verse 14). Yet it seems that the Gentiles are perfectly content and quite happy, now that God's glory is revealed. In other places it is said that they will have a share in Israel's religion, and pray and offer sacrifice: Isa. 56. 6–8, 66. 18–21, Psalm 86. 8–10.

It is not said that the Jews are to go out into all lands as missionaries. The coming in of the Gentiles is seen as a movement to a centre. The Sanctuary at Jerusalem is the centre of Israel's unity; it is to become the centre of unity for mankind.

Therefore it is always to Jerusalem that the Gentiles come. They are seen moving towards the Centre. This is the case in the earliest prophecy on this subject (Isa. 2. 2–4):

'The mountain of the LORD's house shall be established in the top of the mountains
And shall be exalted above the hills,
    And all nations shall flow unto it.
And many peoples shall say,
Come ye, and let us go up to the mountain of the LORD
    To the house of the God of Jacob;
And he will teach us of his ways,
And we will walk in his paths;
For out of Zion shall go forth the Law,
And the word of the LORD from Jerusalem.'

We shall see, when we come to the Fulfilment, how the principle holds good; for however far the missionaries go, they are calling men to come to the Centre of Unity, which is Christ (pp. 139–40 below).

REDEMPTION THROUGH SUFFERING

One more point remains to be considered, in the exilic prophecies of the LORD's future action; the four poems of the Servant of the LORD in Isaiah 40–55. It has been a matter of much discussion who the Servant is. In the first two at least, the Servant is Israel, and this is explicit in the second poem, 49. 3, 5; the poems depict Israel's vocation. The same seems to be true of the third, which shows the Servant patiently enduring suffering and trusting in God. But the fourth poem goes so deep and its range is so wide, that what is described in it can be no less than the salvation of mankind; it seems that we are forced to say that the prophet is thinking of One who should come. His work is described as an accepted sacrifice (53. 10) and redemptive suffering by which sin is overcome and taken away (53. 11–12).

In the first poem (42. 1–4), we have a picture of the Servant as the Israelite indeed, rendering to God spiritual service according to his will; not by ways of self-advertisement, but by patient ministry to 'the bruised reed' and 'the smoking wick' growing in grace and not being discouraged, till his witness has been borne to the Gentiles also, and they have listened.

In the second poem (49. 1–6), the Servant himself speaks; he is conscious of a vocation from his birth, and that he is called to be an instrument in the LORD's hand, sharp and effective, to be used to his glory. Tempted to discouragement, when his witness to his own people seems to be in vain, he leaves all to God; and then he is told that his vocation, for which he was called from birth, is not only to gather together the people of Israel to be truly the People of the LORD, but also to be a light to the Gentiles in all parts of the earth.

In the third poem (50. 4–9), the Servant again speaks. It is for him to be a disciple, waiting morning by morning for the LORD's word, with a sensitive ear; and he has followed this way obediently, in spite of cruel persecution which he has patiently endured, trusting in the LORD to vindicate him.

In the fourth poem, the Servant is not the speaker, but others speak about him—indeed they can do no else than speak about him. It consists of five stanzas, in each of which the first phrase gives the theme of the stanza, and is here printed in italics.

In the first stanza God speaks: *His Servant* (taken as known from the other poems) *shall prosper* (i.e. prevail, as one who 'deals wisely' and, as we say, makes good); he shall be vindicated by God, though many have been shocked at him, and misunderstood his suffering (52. 12–15).

In the second stanza (53. 1–3), the people speak (perhaps Gentiles, perhaps Israelites; it is best to leave it indefinite, as 'we'): '*Who among us believed what we were told?*' We saw the LORD's Servant suffer, and we despised him.

In the third (53. 4–6), the people again speak: Now we understand; it was *the pain and suffering which we deserved* that *he was bearing*. He was suffering for us. It was we who had offended, going astray like lost sheep. He bore it all.

In the fourth (53. 7–9), the prophet speaks, interpreting the meaning further. The LORD's Servant *was oppressed*, patiently enduring cruelty practised on him (verse 7), suffering condemnation through miscarriage of justice (verse 8), and dying a martyr's death (verse 9).

In the fifth stanza (53. 10–12), the prophet speaks in God's Name, till in verses 11 and 12 it is God himself speaking: 'In all this *God's own work of salvation is seen*; the Servant's martyrdom is an accepted sacrifice, and the end shall be blessing and peace. His soul shall be satisfied, when he sees how the souls of men have been saved from the power of evil. The LORD's Servant is a great conqueror, through having given up his life unto death, being counted as a wrong-doer, and in all this bearing the sin of men and praying for them.

But this fifth stanza must be quoted in full:

> 'Yet it pleased the LORD to bruise him;
> He hath made him sick;
>   When thou shalt make his soul a guilt-offering,
> He shall see his seed,
> He shall prolong his days,
> And the pleasure of the LORD shall prosper in his hand.
> "He shall see of the travail of his soul,
>   And shall be satisfied.
> By his knowledge shall my righteous Servant justify many;
>   And he shall bear their iniquities.
> Therefore will I divide him a portion with the great
> And he shall divide the spoil with the strong,
> Because he poured out his soul unto death,
> And was numbered with the transgressors,
> Yet he bare the sin of many,
> And made intercession for the transgressors." '

In 1 Peter 1. 10–11 we have what must certainly be a direct commentary on Isaiah 53:

'The prophets who prophesied of the grace that was to be yours searched and enquired about this salvation; they inquired what person or time was indicated by the Spirit of Christ within them when predicting the sufferings of Christ and the subsequent glory. It was revealed to them that they were serving not themselves but you, in the things which have now been announced to you by those who preached the good news to you.' (*R.S.V. translation.*)

CHAPTER IX

'Rejoice ye with Jerusalem'

HAGGAI, ZECHARIAH, NEHEMIAH, EZRA

Dates

Cyrus captures Babylon	538
Sheshbazzar's return	538
Rebuilding of the Temple	520–16
Nehemiah's return	444
Ezra's return perhaps	428

THE HISTORY OF THIS PERIOD

THE period of the later Exile was one in which things of great importance were happening, and yet there is no written history. We are now in a position to answer the question, why they never wrote the history of the Exile, as they wrote the history (in itself less important) of the Kings of Judah and Israel. It was because they needed to study the pre-exilic history, in order to know how they had sinned and had incurred God's just punishment. Nothing was more important than that they should repent of that sin, and avoid it for the future. Of their life in Babylon, there was nothing to record: better forget it: oh, that it might soon be over! For the time was coming (oh, that it might be soon!) when history would begin again, when the LORD God would take action to redeem his people. Then there would be a new Book of the Exodus to write.

So it is that there is no biblical history of the Exilic period, and only the very fragmentary history in Ezra and Nehemiah down to about 400, and then none at all till the Maccabees. But the words of the LORD spoken by the prophets were preserved and treasured: Isaiah 56–66, dating from the period after 538 B.C.; Haggai and Zechariah 1–8, concerned with the rebuilding of the Temple; Malachi, dating from about 450, shortly before Nehemiah; Jonah, dating from after Ezra. So also there were many additions to the Psalms used in

97

temple and synagogue. But most of all they were concerned to go back to their wonderful past, and produce the 'Priestly' version of the narratives of Genesis and Exodus and the Laws in Leviticus and Numbers.

In this period of the Return from Exile the whole stimulus came from the zealous and disciplined community in Babylonia. But those of them who returned to the devastated homeland found a most difficult and discouraging task awaiting them.

THE REBUILDING OF THE TEMPLE

Cyrus and the Persian kings who followed him reversed the cruel policy of the Assyrian and Babylonian empires towards the subject peoples. The downfall of both these had been hailed with shouts of joy: that of Assyria by the prophet Nahum about 612 B.C., that of Babylon in Isa 13 and 14. 1–23 (cf. Ps. 137). Second Isaiah had seen what was coming; and Cyrus did in fact allow the subject peoples to develope their own cultures, provided that the peace of the world from Asia Minor and Egypt to the borders of India was not disturbed. Thus there is no reason to doubt that he made a decree that the Jews might rebuild the Temple at Jerusalem (Ezra 1. 1–4).

Thus in 538 or soon after a band of devoted and stalwart men, led by Sheshbazzar (Ezra 1. 9, 11), set out on the long journey home; they rebuilt the altar for the sacrifices (3. 2–6), and in the following year laid the foundations of the Temple, with very great joy (3. 10–13).

But difficulties arose. It seems that no one in Babylon had understood in what desolation the land of Judaea was, with the towns destroyed and the trees cut down, and how poverty-stricken the people were. This has been confirmed by the archaeologists, who have found that one town-site after another remained in ruins for two hundred years and more. (See W. F. Albright, *The Archaeology of Palestine*, Penguin, 1947, pp. 140–2). Haggai makes clear how great the poverty of the people was when the work of rebuilding began to go forward in 520. Another difficulty also arose; the people of Samaria (a mixed population, partly Israelites and partly Mesopotamians brought thither by the Assyrian king after the Fall of Samaria in 721, 2 Kings 17. 24–41) made objections to any temple-building at Jerusalem, Ezra 4. 1–5 and 24, and the work ceased till the reign of Darius which began in 520 B.C.

But in spite of all difficulties, the work was carried through, Ezra 5 and 6. The leaders saw how necessary it was that the believing and worshipping community should have its Temple. Further, it seemed that the LORD's time was at hand, for the date was now 520, and the 'seventy years' of which Jeremiah had spoken (Jer. 25. 12, 29. 10) as the time of the Exile were nearly up; and this seemed to be confirmed by the fact that the Persian empire was in turmoil, and Darius was having great difficulties in suppressing revolts against his rule.

It seems also that there were great hopes that the Davidic kingdom was to be restored, in the person of Zerubbabel, who was of the old royal line. He was working with the two prophets in the temple-building (Hag. 1. 1, 12, 2. 1–9). It is possible that Zerubbabel was actually crowned as king, but we do not know for certain; and our sources seem to be in some little confusion. If the attempt was actually made to restore the Davidic kingdom, it certainly failed altogether. Certainly this was not to be the promised Day of the LORD, nor was the way of temporal kingship his way.

NEHEMIAH AND EZRA

The work of Nehemiah and Ezra marks the next stage in the history. The Temple had been built, but if we may judge from the prophecy of Malachi, which is usually dated about 450 B.C., the worship of the community was then exceedingly slack and slovenly. Blind and lame animals were good enough to offer in sacrifice! The Persian governor could not be treated like that! (Mal. 1. 8). There is much more of the same kind (2. 1–10, 10–17). The prophet seeks to instil a wholesome fear of the LORD: He must be taken seriously!

After Nehemiah and Ezra had done their work, these things no longer happened. Nehemiah was a layman, Ezra an ecclesiastic, 'a ready scribe in the Law of Moses' (Ezra 7. 6); but both were of one mind in their zeal for the LORD, and both were representatives of the community of the faithful in Babylonia. Nehemiah's work was to rebuild the walls of Jerusalem, as Governor of the province; Ezra's, to promulgate the 'Priestly Law' and thereby to inaugurate the Reformed Judaism which from this time on held the field in Israel.

It has been for a long time a debated question, which of them came first; it is a complicated historical problem, in which only the opinion of an expert is of real value. On the face of things, it would seem that the building of the walls should come before the regulation of worship; and in the most recent and the best book on Old Testament history, Dr. John Bright's *History of Israel* (1960), it is held that Nehemiah did indeed come first, about 444 (Neh. 2. 1) and stayed till 433 (13. 6), and returned a little later (13. 7); Ezra came about 428, and he and Nehemiah were together at the Promulgation of the Law (Neh. 8. 9 and 10. 1).

Nehemiah tells in his memoirs (Neh. 1 and 2) of the call that came to him to go to Jerusalem. In 2. 11–20 there is his thrilling account of his moonlight survey of the ruined walls; in chapter 3, of the work of wall-building, and in the next three chapters, of his determined and very able conduct of these operations, amid constant peril from Samaritan and other enemies, who greatly desired that Jerusalem should remain defenceless. He did a great work, and showed great courage in the doing of it; see for instance Neh. 6. 1–9 and 10–14.

Next in Nehemiah's memoirs comes the account of the Promulgation of the Law, in which Ezra took the lead, in chapters 8, 9, and 10; and here, as we have seen, Nehemiah's name also appears. The last chapter of the book, chapter 13, is concerned chiefly with the unpleasant subject of mixed marriages of Jewish husbands with pagan wives, of which there will be more to be said later; Ezra also took his part in dealing with this, as is related in Ezra's memoirs, in Ezra 9 and 10.

EZRA'S REFORM

In Nehemiah chapters 8–10 is it very evidently a great occasion that is being described, comparable to the Covenant under king

Josiah almost two hundred years earlier, in 2 Kings 23. Ezra stands in a wooden pulpit, flanked by Levites on either side, and reads to the people from early morning till midday out of 'The book of the Law of Moses which the LORD commanded to Israel' (8. 1)— which he had brought from Babylon, Ezra 7. 14—and he praises the LORD, and all the people answer 'Amen' (Neh. 8. 3–6). The Levites explain the Law to the people. After this they keep the Feast of Booths or Tabernacles with great gladness, according to the instructions in Leviticus 23 (8. 13–20).

Three weeks later a solemn Covenant is made. A solemn liturgical prayer is pronounced by the Levites, or according to the Greek Bible (LXX) by Ezra *solo* (9. 5–38). In it the LORD is praised for his mighty acts: the creation, the call of Abraham, the Exodus and the law-giving at Sinai, the manna in the wilderness, the conquest of Canaan; with this goes the confession of the national sin, from the Golden Calf at Sinai onwards, in their continual disobedience to the word of the LORD spoken by the prophets. For this he has visited them with his judgements; but he has not forsaken them. 'Now therefore', verse 32, in their present sad condition as subjects of a pagan empire, they call upon him and make a sure Covenant. The list of those who sign it is headed by Nehemiah, 10. 1.

This prayer in Neh. 9 is possibly the noblest instance the Old Testament of the 'Theology of Recital' (pp. 8–9 above). In being addressed to God, it is on the same pattern as the great Eucharistic Prayers in the ancient Greek liturgies of the Church, notably those of 'St. Basil' and 'St. James'.

So they sign and seal the Covenant, undertaking 'to walk in God's Law which was given by Moses the servant of God, and to observe and do all the commandments of the LORD our God and his judgements and his statutes' (10. 29), not entering into mixed marriages (30), keeping the Sabbath (31), and accepting a fixed charge to pay for the Temple services, with offerings of firstfruits of crops and cattle (32–39).

Yet it is not clear precisely what the document was which was thus 'canonized': whether it was the 'Priestly' Law, or the Mosaic Law as a whole, or the Pentateuch as whole, which included narrative as well as law. But in any case the Mosaic Law as it stands in the Pentateuch now became binding; it was the inauguration of post-exilic Judaism. The importance of Ezra in the history is attested by the great place which he has taken in Jewish tradition, and by the legends which gathered round his name. There is a queer story in a book of the Apocrypha that all the books of the Law and the Prophets, indeed the whole Old Testament, were destroyed at the Fall of Jerusalem, and the whole was miraculously revealed to him and by him written out (2 Esdras 14. 37–48).

The truth that lies behind this legend seems to be that Ezra was responsible for the canonization of the five 'Books of the Law', as we have them, from Genesis to Deuteronomy. Ever after, the 'five books of Moses' held the place of honour in the Old Testament; they were acknowledged as Scripture by some who did not accept the rest of the Old Testament (the Sadducees in our LORD's day, and the Samaritans who went into schism some time in the fourth century). These were now 'Scripture'.

In addition, there were the words of the LORD by the prophets: that is to say, first the 'historical' books from Joshua to 2 Kings, which are still printed in Hebrew Bibles as 'the Earlier Prophets'; then the 'Later Prophets', Isaiah, Jeremiah and Ezekiel (not Daniel), and 'the Twelve', namely what we usually call the 'minor prophets'. These were reckoned as Scripture by the time of Ben-Sira (Ecclesiasticus), about 180 B.C., as we see in his summary of the contents of his Bible, Ecclus. chapters 44–49.

The third part of the Hebrew Bible consists of the 'Writings': the Psalms, Job, the Proverbs, Daniel, the Chronicles and the other books in our Bible. This threefold division of the Old Testament is reflected in Luke 24. 44, 'the Law of Moses, and the Prophets, and the Psalms'.

This the Covenant of Ezra marks the foundation of 'Judaism'. It stands as a great confession of faith. Josiah's Covenant had been made shortly before Israel entered on its agony of suffering and death: Ezra's, after it had come out alive.

THE 'PRIESTLY' NARRATIVES AND LAWS

Because the God of Israel was the God who had acted in history, its Bible had to be a historical record. Yet the biblical history is a different sort of history from the 'scientific' history which is written today, and which engages in 'a disinterested search for knowledge for its own sake', and in its history-writing sets out to determine 'exactly what happened' and to reconstruct an 'objective' outline of the actual course of the events.

Yet it is to be doubted whether any human history-writing can be wholly 'objective' and 'without bias'; for we who write it are ourselves engaged in shaping the history of our own day, and therefore we see the events of the past from our own point of view. Thus there are humanistically-minded historians who are interested in tracing man's intellectual progress, or again the evolution of his religious ideas; and there are patriotic historians such as those who produced the older type of school-histories of England, to show the glory of the British Empire. Likewise there is much difference between Catholic and Protestant histories of the Reformation. Such 'bias', whether secularist or patriotic or denominational, shows itself in the judgements which are pronounced on the facts.

That the biblical history-writing has a 'bias' cannot be denied; but it is a bias that is all its own. The biblical writers are not concerned to glorify man, or to glorify Israel; they tell the story as the record of the works of the LORD, beginning with his action in creating his world, and going on to his acts of salvation and judgement in his dealings with Israel. Hence biblical history-writing includes the confession of man's sin.

Certainly the truth of the facts is important; the record of God's acts in history will be false if the facts recorded are not true. And here it is possible to accuse the biblical historians generally and the 'priestly' writers in particular of distorting the facts. Did Methusaleh really live to the age of 969? Was Moses eighty years of age at the Exodus, and did 600,000 Israelite men, besides their women and children, come out of Egypt? Or again, the Tabernacle in the wilderness could scarcely have been transported from place to place without a fleet of lorries with caterpillar tracks.

Yet the 'priestly' writers who gave us these details did have a sense of history. We ought to set it to their credit that they preserved the text of the earlier-written narratives side by side with their own narratives, which probably they liked better. There was a genuine historical conscientiousness here. It must be added also that modern biblical scholars, unlike those of the nineteenth century, are finding authentic historical information not given in the older stories, at many points in the 'priestly' narratives, and many quite ancient ordinances in the 'priestly' laws.

We have said that their view of history begins with the action of God in creating his world. And as we noticed on pages 2–3 above, the first eleven chapters of Genesis do not mention Israel at all; they are concerned with mankind, and the Covenant with Noah in chapter 9 speaks of the Divine ordinances to which all men are subject.

When they tell the story of the Exodus, they tell it as men who have a share in the Exodus, as their annual Passover testifies:

'And thou shalt tell thy son in that day, saying, It is because of that which the LORD did *for me when I* came forth out of Egypt. And it shall be for a sign unto thee upon thine hand, and for a memorial between thine eyes, that the law of the LORD may be in thy mouth; for with a strong hand hath the LORD *brought thee* out of Egypt'. (Exod. 13. 8–9.)

We Christians should understand this, for we sing at Christmas, 'O come ye, O come ye to Bethlehem'.

Similarly when they write about the Tabernacle in the wilderness, they describe it as a model of the Temple at which they themselves worship, for they are thinking of the continuity and the unity of their own faith with that of Moses. Their thoughts go back to the LORD's 'wonders of old time' in the distant past, and forward to the future Day when he would visit and redeem his people, and his visible Presence would return to fill the Temple with his Glory, and give his people one heart and one mind in serving him. Christians should understand this, for our own thoughts go back to the events of our redemption in the past, and upward to the ascended Lord, and forward to the consummation of his purpose in the future.

Similarly their law of worship and of daily life was to them the Law of Moses. Moses had in fact been the historical founder of Israel's law, as we have seen in chapter IV; and the ordinances which had been added later had been designed to adapt the Mosaic principles to new conditions. This must have begun as soon as Israel entered Canaan and learnt the arts of agriculture; it continued when Israel began to have kings and to be a civilized nation; near the end of the Monarchy the Code of Deuteronomy summed all this up, and showed what we can call a blue-print of a national life under the rule of God. The 'priestly' revision in turn is a new edition of an old tradition, and is rightly seen as 'the Law of Moses' because of the continuity of the nation's faith. In a sense, Moses was still speaking to them. There is an excellent study of this in the booklet entitled *Moses* by Professor von Rad of Heidelberg in the World Dominion series, 1960.

At the same time, as we shall see in the next two chapters, the codification of Law brought with it the peril of the substitution of law-keeping for real obedience to God.

JUDAISM AND THE GENTILE WORLD

Similar considerations will throw light on the 'purges' in which Nehemiah and Ezra turned adrift numbers of women from surrounding countries who in all innocence had married Jewish husbands. We read in Neh. 13. 24 of wives from Ashdod, Ammon, and Moab: ' and their children spake half in the language of Ashdod, and could not speak in the Jews' language, but according to the language of each people'. The same was brought to Ezra's notice when he first came into the country (Ezra 9. 1–3); and it nearly broke his heart. We can read in his memoirs his agonized and shame-stricken prayer. This was the very sin for which God had visited his people with that terrible punishment. And now, when it seemed that Israel was penitent and forgiven, and there was real hope of a new start, there had come this awful relapse, on the part even of some who had returned from exile (9. 4).

At the evening oblation I arose up from my humiliation, even with my garment and my mantle rent; and I fell upon my knees, and spread out my hands unto the LORD my God; and I said:

'O my God, I am ashamed and blush to lift up my face to thee, my God: for our iniquities are increased over our head, and our guiltiness is grown up to the heavens. Since the days of our fathers we have been exceedingly guilty, unto this day. . . . And now for a little moment grace hath been showed from the LORD our God, to leave us a remnant to escape, and to give us a nail in his holy place, that our God may lighten our eyes, and give us a little reviving in our bondage. . . . And now, O our God, what shall we say after this? for we have forsaken thy commandments, which thou hast commanded by thy servants the prophets. . . . And after all that is come upon us for our evil deeds, . . . shall we again break thy commandments, and join in affinity with the peoples that do these abominations? Wouldest thou not be angry with us till thou hadst consumed us, so that there should be no remnant, nor any to escape? (Ezra 9. 5–15.)

For the Israelite's home was the place where the children were to be taught in the ways of the LORD (Deut. 6. 7): repeatedly in the Law it is said that the children would ask, for instance, about the Passover, 'What mean ye by this service?' But now paganism was being admitted into the home itself; pagan mothers, knowing no better, would bring up the children in a pagan way. There was no help for it: this evil must be stopped at once, however painful the process. In Ezra 10 we read how they spent days and days going into individual cases. Nehemiah, it is to be feared, had been far less patient (Neh. 13. 25, 28).

It was a painful duty, but it had to be done. Yet questions rise. Had not the Second Isaiah spoken a century or more earlier, of the conversion of the Gentiles to believe in the God of Israel? Does this turning adrift of the Gentile wives mean that there had been a sad falling-away from that earlier ideal? Then, Israel was to stretch out its arms and include the Gentiles: now, it was busy pushing them away and excluding them.

There was something in this. The author of the *Book of Jonah*, writing perhaps not long after Ezra, bitterly satirizes the Jews of his day for their harsh attitude towards the Gentiles.

In this tale Jonah, though commanded to speak in God's name to the people of Nineveh, takes ship in the opposite direction, to the far west (1. 1–3). God sends a violent storm; in the storm, the pagan sailors show up much better than Jonah; they pray to their respective gods, while he retires to his bunk to sleep (verses 5, 6). He has told them that he is running away from God, and that they will have to throw him overboard; they row hard in order not to have to do this, but at last Jonah has to go. The storm at once moderates; the men 'feared the LORD exceedingly, and they offered a sacrifice to the LORD, and made vows' (1. 10–16). Clearly there was good in these Gentiles. As for Jonah, he must now resume his errand (3. 1–3); the result is a remarkable response on the part of the Ninevites (3. 4–10). Jonah is disgusted, and tells God so:

But it displeased Jonah exceedingly, and he was angry. And he prayed unto the LORD, and said, 'I pray thee, O LORD, was not this my saying, when I was yet in my country? Therefore I hasted to flee to Tarshish; for I knew that thou art a gracious God and full of compassion, slow to anger, and plenteous in mercy, and repentest thee of the evil.' (4. 1–2.)

Finally, peevish and petulant Jonah is annoyed because the gourd which shelters him perishes; but if Jonah is grieved about the gourd, on which he has bestowed no labour, shall not God care about the people of Nineveh who are his own creatures? (4. 10–11.)

The *Book of Ruth* also was probably written, or re-edited, about this time; we can see signs of this, e.g. in 4. 7.

Deuteronomy had said that an Ammonite or Moabite must not enter into the assembly of the LORD, to the tenth generation (Deut. 23. 3), and the prohibition was quoted and used by Nehemiah (13. 1, 2). But this charming tale of Ruth tells of the good and faithful Moabite woman who marries an Israelite husband, and becomes the great-grandmother of no less a person than David himself (Ruth 4. 17.)

But here is the strange thing. The faith of Israel that the LORD God of Israel is the one true God leads to two opposite conclusions. He alone is God: therefore all nations whom he has made must come at last to worship him (Isa. 45. 22–23; Ps. 86. 9–10). He alone

H

is God: therefore Israel which he has called to know him, must beware lest it be drawn away from him into idolatry (cf. the First Commandment). An idolatrous and paganized Israel would deserve God's judgement (Ezra 9. 13–14), and would be of no use in witnessing for God to the Gentiles.

We ought not then to blame Nehemiah and Ezra for losing sight of the noble 'universalism' of Second Isaiah, as if it were simply a matter of ecclesiastical narrow-mindedness. If they and their successors had been broad-minded, tolerant and lax, their Judaism would have lost its cutting edge, and have lost at the same time its power to attract the Gentiles. For here was a religion which was exclusive because it believed in a Real God, who had made a Covenant with his People, and imposed on them a weekly Sabbathday, and abstinence from forbidden foods, and a high moral demand; and at the same time a God whom it proclaimed as the Creator and the God of the whole earth.

Israel was being pulled in two directions at once. The problem of the Gentile world was one which it could not solve. No solution was possible till the Messiah had come, and God's Purpose for Israel had been completed.

CHAPTER X

'Lord, what love have I unto Thy Law'

ISRAEL UNDER GREEK AND ROMAN RULE

Dates

Alexander overthrows the Persian Empire,	334–323
Israel ruled from Egypt (the Ptolemies) till	200
thereafter from Syria (the Seleucids) till	167
The Maccabean revolt	166
Maccabean high-priests	160—63
Pompey in Palestine; Roman rule	63 onwards
Herod the Great as vassal-king	40–4 B.C.

IN the last stage of the Old Testament story, Israel became subject, no longer to Oriental empires, but to those of the West, Greece and Rome. Israel had for a century or so been in contact with Greek culture; the coins of Athens, with an owl embossed on them, had circulated freely. But the change of rule came suddenly, with the lightning campaigns of Alexander the Great, who had crossed into Asia in 334 and within seven years had advanced to the Indus, having destroyed the main Persian army at Issus in 333, captured impregnable Tyre and received the submission of Egypt in 332, overthrown the Persian empire at Arbela in 331 and taken the capital cities. He died in 323 at the age of thirty-five; his generals ruled in his stead, Ptolemy in Egypt, where Alexandria was now founded, and Seleucus in Syria and Mesopotamia, where the other great Greek city of Antioch now began.

Of these great events there is no mention at all in the Hebrew Bible. Israel was a people apart, and to the life and worship at Jerusalem the change of rulers made little difference. Yet we shall see in this chapter how this nation, so different from the other nations, was nevertheless profoundly influenced by attraction to and repulsion from this new Western culture.

THE TEMPLE WORSHIP

The Book of Chronicles, of which Ezra and Nehemiah form a continuation, was till lately dated about 300 B.C., but reasons are now given for dating it a century earlier, about 400, and so only twenty or thirty years after Ezra's Reform. But it makes little difference; for the reformed temple worship was going on throughout this period.

Chronicles is a history of Israel from the beginning, but the telling of the story begins with David's reign, in 1 Chron. 10. It is a 'priestly' history, largely reproducing the account in Samuel and Kings, but adding some authentic historical information, and greatly elaborating the liturgical details; also, because for our author 'Samaria' means 'the Samaritans' of his day, the story of the northern kingdom is almost completely passed over. His military history is often fantastic, as in 2 Chron. 13; Israel in his day had no army.

But his liturgical writing is wonderful. The following is an act of praise, put into the mouth of David:

> 'Blessed be thou, O LORD,
> The God of Israel our Father,
>   For ever and ever.
> Thine, O LORD, is the greatness, and the power,
> And the glory, and the victory, and the majesty:
>   For all that is in the heaven and in the earth is thine:
> For thine is the Kingdom, O Lord,
> And thou art exalted as head above all.
> Both riches and honour come of thee,
> And in thine hand is power and might,
> And in thine hand it is to make great,
>   And to give strength unto all.
> Now therefore, our God, we thank thee
>   And praise thy glorious Name.
> But who am I, and what is my people,
> That we should be able to offer so willingly after this sort?
>   For all things come of thee,
>   And of thine own have we given thee.' (1 Chron. 29. 10–14.)

There is another splendid piece which describes the bringing of the Sacred Ark into Solomon's temple at its dedication. It is not merely that our author describes that liturgical action 'as it ought to have been done'; we should reckon that what he is really thinking of is the great future event of the Return of the LORD's visible presence to his sanctuary, at the coming Day of Salvation:

'It came to pass, when the priests were come out of the Holy Place ... also the Levites which were the singers, all of them ... arrayed in fine linen, with cymbals and psalteries and harps, stood at the east end of the altar, and with them a hundred and twenty priests sounding with trumpets; it came even to pass, when the trumpeters and singers were as one, to make one sound in praising and thanking the LORD; and when they lifted up their voice with the trumpets and cymbals and instruments of music, and praised the LORD, saying
> "For he is good:
> For his mercy endureth for ever",

that then the House was filled with a Cloud, even the House of the LORD, so that the priests could not stand to minister by reason of the Cloud; for the Glory of the LORD filled the House of God.' (2 Chron. 5. 11–14.)

THE DIVINE WISDOM

For centuries 'the wise man' had commanded great respect all over the Middle East, as for instance in Egypt, Edom, Arabia; Solomon had been a great man of wisdom, and some of the material in the Book of Proverbs may well be his. But the pursuit of Wisdom received a fresh stimulus when Israel came into contact with Greek men of wisdom.

It is commonly held that the Book of Proverbs was edited in the Greek period, and that the first nine chapters were written then. To the Israelite writer, Wisdom is not a human quality merely, not a personification of 'Education'; she is the Divine Wisdom, God's voice speaking to man and apprehended by his reason and conscience. She existed from the first creation of the world, and was in God's Mind when he laid the foundations of the earth. Therefore whoever rejects the voice of Wisdom sins against his own true being:

> The LORD possessed me in the beginning of His way,
> Before his works of old.
> I was set up from everlasting, from the beginning,
> Before ever the world was . . .
>> When he established the heavens, I was there,
>> When he set a circle upon the face of the deep . . .
>> When he gave to the sea its bound,
>> That the waters should not transgress his commandment;
>> When he marked out the foundations of the earth,
> Then I was by him, as a master-workman,
> And I was daily his delight,
> Rejoicing always before him,
> Rejoicing in his habitable earth,
>> And my delight was with the sons of men.
> Now therefore, my sons, hearken unto me,
> For blessed are they that keep my ways. (Prov. 8. 22–32.)

Here indeed something is being said. As in Babylon the author of Genesis, chapter 1, had produced an epic of creation, so in contact with this new Greek world they return to this theme of creation. The Greek nation had produced the philosophers, who had speculated about the origin of things, and laid the foundations of natural science. To them this teaching about the divine Wisdom would appeal, when the Jew met them in Alexandria.

There was also another side to it. The first seven chapters of Proverbs contain a series of fervent moral exhortations, addressed to the Jewish young man surrounded on every side with new temptations to immorality which met him in the free life of the Greek city. These chapters are not occupied with 'conventional morals'; they were written to meet the urgent need of young men in great moral danger:

> 'My son, if thou wilt receive my words,
> And lay up my commandments with thee,
> So that thou incline thine ear unto wisdom,
> And apply thine heart to understanding . . .
> Then thou shalt understand the fear of the LORD,
> And find the knowledge of God . . .
> For wisdom shall enter into thine heart,

And knowledge shall be pleasant unto thy soul . . .
To deliver thee from the way of evil,
From the men that speak froward things,
Who forsake the paths of uprightness
To walk in the ways of darkness . . .
To deliver thee from the strange woman,
Even from the stranger that flattereth with her words,
Which forsaketh the friend of her youth,
And forgetteth the Covenant of her God;
For her house inclineth unto death,
And her paths unto the dead:
None that go to her return again,
Neither do they attain to the paths of life.' (Prov. 2. 1–19.)

In the Hebrew Bible, 'Wisdom' never means 'reason', scientific inquiry, logical analysis. It has this meaning in the *Wisdom of Solomon* in the Apocrypha, a book written in Greek in the first century B.C.; there, in 7. 17–20, it is said that Wisdom has taught man physics and astronomy, zoology, meteorology, botany and medicine. But in the Hebrew books it is never so. The point is summed up in Job 28. 28:

'And unto man He said,
"Behold, the fear of the LORD, that is wisdom;
And to depart from evil is understanding." '

But we cannot here pursue this subject further. We will only add that the phrases used in the Prologue to St. John's gospel, 1. 1–18, show that the idea of Wisdom, *Sophia*, forms part of what St. John means by 'the Word', the *Logos*. As the divine Wisdom is God's voice speaking to man, and apprehended by his mind and conscience, so in Jesus is seen the true pattern of human nature, whereby man is delivered from the dominion of Satan and of his selfish pride.

FAITHFULNESS UNTO DEATH

Judaism had a different sort of contact with Greek thought when Antiochus Epiphanes ('the Magnificent') sought to impose throughout Syria and the countries dependent on Antioch a uniform pattern of Greek civilization: 'that all should be on people, and that each should forsake his own laws' (1 Macc. 1. 41–42). The programme was accepted everywhere. It was attractive, it was up-to-date; and among the peoples of the Middle East only one found any sufficient reason for refusing to march in the path of progress. If it meant building temples and offering sacrifice to an additional god or two in addition to those already worshipped, what of that? Where there are many gods, there is always room for one more: except only in Israel.

For there was one nation which believed in one God only, and that he was the true God, and had called Israel to be his People—and that it mattered. The New Order required that in the Temple set apart for his worship sacrifices should be offered to Zeus and Aphrodite, the Sabbath be disregarded, the food-rules of the Law be set aside (1 Macc. 1. 44–49); besides, all sorts of strange foreign customs were brought in, a Greek Gymnasium or sports-ground was made, and all the traditions of Israel's life were broken. For the New Order, so generously tolerant of all religions, could not tolerate a religion which men treated seriously because it rested on the worship of the one true God.

Hence a systematic persecution began: heathen altars appeared everywhere in Palestine, copies of the Book of the Law were confiscated and burnt, and those who refused to conform, and women who had their babies circumcised, were put to death.

'And many in Israel were fully resolved and confirmed in themselves, not to eat unclean things; and they chose to die, that they might not be defiled with the meats, and that they might not profane the holy covenant: and they died.' (1 Macc. 1. 62–63.)

Some of them fled into the wilderness; the king's forces pursued them there, and prepared to attack them on the Sabbath day, first offering amnesty and free pardon if even now they would conform: they refused, and a thousand, including women and children, were massacred on one day (2. 29–38). There is another story in 2 Macc. 6. 18–17, of seven sons of one mother, who gave their lives, one after another, as martyrs for the faith. There followed the armed rising under Judas Maccabeus, a heroic struggle in which a succession of foreign armies were defeated, and an independent Jewish state set up.

This persecution and these martyrdoms appear to be alluded to in the splendid panegyric on the heroes of the faith in Heb. 11. 33–38; a passage which was an unconscious prophecy of the persecutions of the Christians which began about the time when the Epistle to the Hebrews was written, and continued, on and off, for 250 years, till at last the victory was won and the Roman Empire became Christian:

'Who through faith subdued kingdoms, wrought righteousness, obtained promises, stopped the mouths of lions [like Daniel], quenched the power of fire [like the Three Children in Dan. 3], escaped the edge of the sword, from weakness were made strong, waxed mighty in war, put to flight armies of aliens [like Judas Maccabeus]. Women received their dead by a resurrection: and others were tortured, not accepting their deliverance, that they might obtain a better resurrection; and others had trial of mockings and scourgings, yea moreover of bonds and imprisonment; they were stoned, they were sawn asunder, they were tempted, they were slain with the sword: they went about in sheepskins and goatskins, being destitute, afflicted, evil entreated (of whom the world was not worthy) wandering in deserts and mountains and caves, and the holes of the earth.' (Heb. 11. 33–38.)

The first of the persecutions was this Maccabean persecution. Now we see another side of the 'exclusiveness' which we were discussing in the last chapter. Loyalty to faith in the one true God made this exclusiveness necessary. Now the test came; and Israel was found faithful, even unto death.

One book of the Old Testament belongs to this period, and was written to sustain the faith of the martyrs in their conflict: the Book of Daniel. This book purports to be a story of events in the time of Nebuchadnezzar, four hundred years before: but its actual reference is to this persecution. The great story of the Burning Fiery Furnace was written to describe the New Order which Antiochus Epiphanes set up, to which all peoples, nations, and languages were required to conform under pain of death (Dan. 3. 4–6). The style of this chapter is purposely formal and stilted; we can discern a tone of mockery in the enumeration of the state officials and civil servants, and that of the musical instruments—both repeated several times; but the grim reality behind them is that of the totalitarian state and a culture imposed by threat of force:

'Nebuchadnezzar the king made an image of gold, whose height was threescore cubits [88 feet] and the breadth thereof six cubits [9 feet]; he set it up in the plain of Dura, in the province of Babylon. Then Nebuchadnezzar the king sent to gather together the satraps, the deputies, and the governors, the judges, the treasurers, the counsellors, the sheriffs, and all the rulers of the provinces, to come to the dedication of the image which Nebuchadnezzar the king had set up . . . Then the herald cried aloud, "To you it is commanded, O peoples, nations and languages, that at what time ye hear the sound of the cornet, flute, harp, sackbut, psaltery, dulcimer, and all kinds of music, ye fall down and worship the golden image that Nebuchadnezzar hath set up; and whoso falleth not down and worshippeth shall the same hour be cast into the midst of a burning fiery furnace." ' (Dan. 3. 1–6.)

The three faithful Jews refuse to conform. They say:

'Our God whom we serve is able to deliver us from the burning fiery furnace; and he will deliver us out of thy hand, O king. But if not, be it known unto thee, O king, that we will not worship thy gods, nor worship the golden image which thou hast set up.' (17–18.)

They are then thrown into the furnace (20–23); we are to understand that they died. But the story goes on that they are seen loose, walking in the midst of the fire; and in the midst of the fire there is seen with them Another, and the fire has no power over them (24–28). 'Others were tortured', says the Epistle to the Hebrews, 'not accepting their deliverance, that they might obtain a better resurrection' (Heb. 11. 35).

For it was now that the Jews learnt to believe in the resurrection of the dead. The Old Testament, up to this point, had no clear doctrine of a future life. But these martyrdoms made it clear that those who had loved God enough to lose their lives for his sake, had not lost their lives in losing them, but had found them (Mark 8. 35).

The other chapters of the Book of Daniel all become intelligible in this context. 'Nebuchadnezzar' represents the persecuting heathen power: he boasts of his worldly greatness, saying 'Is not this great Babylon which I have built?' (4. 30). But those whose faith is set in the living God have the secret of a divine kingdom which is real and permanent. In the story of Belshazzar and the Writing on the Wall in chapter 5, judgement is pronounced on the worldly tyrannical power. In chapter 6, Daniel, whose rule of life includes prayer to God three times a day (6. 10; cf. Ps. 55. 17), is thrown to the Den of Lions, and is delivered. In the vision of the Son of Man in chapter 7, there are seen four terrible beasts, representing the world-empires which had oppressed the Israelites, the Assyrian, the Babylonian, the Persian, and lastly the Greek (7. 3–8); but then is seen the throne of God, and a human figure, a son of man:

'I saw in the night visions, and behold, there came with the clouds of heaven one like unto a son of man, and he came even to the Ancient of days, and they brought him near before him. And there was given him dominion, and glory, and a kingdom, that all the peoples, nations and languages should serve him: his dominion is an everlasting dominion, which shall not pass away, and his kingdom that which shall not be destroyed.' (Dan. 7. 13–14.)

Then the vision is explained: the emphasis is all laid on the last and most terrible of the beasts (the persecuting King Antiochus), who will 'make war with the saints and prevail against them' (21), and will 'speak words against the Most High, and he shall think to change the times and the Law; and they shall be given into his hand until a time, and times, and half a time' (25). Those to whom the prophecy is addressed will suffer helplessly; but the matter is in God's hands, and their suffering will be only for as long as he allows. The last word lies with him, and at the last his servants shall possess the Kingdom (26–27).

We should notice here that in Mark 14. 62 our Lord quotes the words of 7–13 in his trial before Caiaphas. He is 'the Son of man'. And the explanation of the vision in 7. 21 and 25 links up with his words in Mark 8. 31, that 'the Son of man must suffer'. But beyond his passion, as that verse shows, lies his resurrection.

THE RIGHTEOUSNESS OF THE LAW

The period of these persecutions saw the beginning of the party of the Pharisees, called 'Assideans' in 1 Macc. 2. 42; faithful men who believed in God and set themselves to discipline their lives according to God's Law. We shall see in the next chapter how they fell under our LORD's judgement; but we shall never understand this unless we see that we ourselves fall under that judgement too.

The wonderful 119th Psalm may have been written perhaps two centuries before the Pharisaic party began to exist; but it expresses perfectly the ideal by which the best Pharisees would have said that they wished to live, and which our Lord endorsed: namely the regulation of all life by obedience to God's will.

> 'Thou has dealt well with thy servant,
> O LORD, according to thy word.
> Teach me good judgment and knowledge;
> For I have believed in thy commandments.
> Before I was afflicted I went astray;
> But now I observe thy word.
> Thou art good, and doest good;
> Teach me thy statutes.' (Ps. 119. 65–68.)

In each of its 176 verses there occurs the word 'law', 'testimonies', 'judgements', or some synonym. Yet this psalm is not legalistic, for it breathes the spirit of a humble and sincere devotion, and expresses delight and joy in seeking to follow the way of God's will. Indeed, this psalm may be said to sum up that which Israel was set to learn above all during the post-exilic period: namely, the personal training-up of the Israelite in the way of the devout life, under the influence of the Synagogue.

If we look back four or five centuries, we can see how great had been the advance. In Babylon, during the Exile, there had been a small remnant of faithful Israelites diligently setting themselves to repent of the sins which the prophets had condemned. A hundred years later, about 450 B.C., Malachi had castigated the slovenliness of the Temple service at Jerusalem: any maimed or lame animal was good enough for sacrifice. Ezra's reforms altered all that; in the later post-exilic period, the Temple sacrifices were performed punctually and reverently. There were synagogues everywhere, in Jerusalem and all over Palestine, and outside Palestine in Babylonia, Egypt, Asia Minor, and all the places where Jews lived: there, Sabbath by Sabbath, the people were instructed in the Law, and trained in habits of devotion. Israel as a whole had become a religious society, with its centre in Jerusalem and its branches spreading far and wide over the world. The old idolatry which the prophets had condemned had ceased to exist. So far as religion was concerned, Israel had become more deeply than ever the People of the LORD; and a great part in this transformation had been played by the patient work of the scribes, who Sabbath by Sabbath had instructed the people in the ways of true religion.

All this was good; but it was fatally spoilt by the readiness of the proud and self-centred heart of man to make a merit of his own good deeds, to compare his own virtues with the faults of others, and to 'make a corner in religion', not rejoicing over the genuine goodness that is seen so often in the lives of quite ungodly people. We ourselves know this same fault in ourselves; and we never understand our Lord's Gospel till we see ourselves as sinners needing forgiveness. We shall have to see in the next chapter how it was the religious people in Israel, and not the 'publicans and sinners' (tax-collectors and prostitutes) who brought him to the death of the cross. This is the paradox of the Gospel: that it was only when man had reached this high level of religious development that he could put this up as a substitute for the real Kingdom or Kingly Rule of God, and so crucify his Saviour. Man does indeed need to be saved from his sinful acts and words and thoughts; but most of all he needs to be saved from the selfish Self.

There is one more point that must be seen before we end this chapter. At the time of the Maccabean persecutions, Judas Maccabaeus saw that it was necessary to fight for the freedom of their faith and worship. There followed the very heroic series of campaigns in which a series of foreign armies were defeated, the Temple which had been desecrated was restored, and an independent Jewish state set up.

It cannot be accidental that in the middle of the next century a series of sacred poems appeared, called the *Psalms of Solomon*—they are not in the Bible—in which the old Messianic Hope of a restored Kingdom of David was revived; for Judas had shown that it was possible for Jewish soldiers to defeat pagan armies, as King David had done. Psalm 17 in this collection set the pattern of the Messianic Hope which the Pharisees believed. The Pharisees themselves did not want another Holy War such as Judas had fought; but there was a right wing of their party, the Zealots, who itched to take up the sword, and in the end did so.

But we must look at part of this psalm:

'Behold, O LORD, and raise up unto them their king, the Son of David, in the time which Thou, O God, knowest, that he may reign over Israel Thy servant;

And gird him with strength that he may break in pieces them that rule unjustly [the Romans] . . .

He shall destroy the ungodly nations with the word of his mouth, so that at his rebuke the nations may flee before him . . .

And he shall gather together a holy people whom he shall lead in righteousness; and he shall judge the tribes of the people that hath been sanctified by the LORD their God.

A righteous king and taught of God is he that reigneth over them; and there shall be no iniquity in his days in their midst; for all shall be holy, and their king is the Lord Messiah.

For he shall not put his trust in horse and rider and bow, nor shall he multiply to himself gold and silver for war [cf. Deut. 17. 16], nor by ships shall he gather confidence for the day of battle.

The LORD himself is his King, and the hope of him that is strong in the hope of God.

And he shall have mercy on the nations that come before him in fear; for he shall smite the earth with the rod of his mouth even for evermore [Isa. 11. 4].

He himself also is free from sin, so that he may make a mighty people, and rebuke princes and overthrow sinners by the might of his word . . . for God shall cause him to be mighty through the Spirit of holiness and wise through the counsel of understanding, with might and righteousness [Isa. 11. 2].

But was the new age, the promised Messianic Reign, to bring forth an Israel devoted to a minute observance of religious rules? And was another side of it to be the imperialism of a nationalistic Israel, ruling other nations with a rod of iron? When we recall the meaning which had been attached by Jeremiah and Ezekiel to the promises of the New Covenant and the outpouring of the Spirit of the LORD, it becomes apparent that this later Judaism had fallen away from that higher vision. It had faithfully preserved the outward forms of its religion; but it had fashioned a notion of the Messiah according to its own ideas, and it was not ready for him whom God would send.

CHAPTER XI

'The Time is fulfilled'

THE GOSPEL

JEW AND CHRISTIAN

A SYMPHONY comes to an end when its themes have all been developed and worked through to their conclusion; a drama comes to an end similarly when the questions which it has asked have been dealt with and some answer has been found. But the Old Testament does not end in any such way. Its questions have been stated, but not answered. There has been the promise that they will be answered by the LORD's future action, but the promise has not been fulfilled. The Messianic Hope remains an unfulfilled hope; men are left waiting for a future Event.

The Jewish view of the Old Testament is that this Messianic Hope still awaits its fulfilment; for that hope, as the Jews of that time understood it, led to the desperate national rebellion against Rome in the Jewish War of A.D. 66–70, which ended in the destruction of the City and the Temple and the end of sacrificial worship. Thereafter a revived Pharisaism settled down to a rigid observance of the Law and the sacred Tradition, in hope of God's future action; and that is still the situation today. The tragedy is that centuries of persecution of Jews by Christians and the anti-Semitism which is still alive today have made it impossible for any but a tiny minority of Jews to accept the Christian answer, that the Old Testament found its fulfilment in Jesus the Messiah. Here is one of the major sins of the Christian Church.

Christians believe that the Messianic Hope of the coming of the Kingdom of God, or God's Kingly Rule, was fulfilled in the person and work of Jesus, even though to the Jew of that day it seemed blasphemous even to think of a 'Messiah crucified'—crucified by those very Romans whom their Messiah ought to have overthrown and triumphed over. Plainly, the Messianic message which the

Apostles proclaimed involved a transformation of the Hope in its historical fulfilment.

We must then say a word about the Fulfilment of Prophecy as the New Testament understands it. Do we take it that prophecy is simple prediction of future events, in such a sense that it is in effect history written in advance? Christians have often interpreted prophecy so. We may take an instance from the narrative of our Lord's crucifixion: his garments were not torn up, but were divided among the squad of soldiers in charge of the execution, and the Scripture was fulfilled which said,

> 'They parted my garments among them,
> And cast lots upon my vesture' (John 19. 24),

the reference being to the dramatic rendering in Ps. 22 of the theme of the Suffering Servant of the LORD in Isa. 53. But are we to infer that the Fulfilment of Prophecy means simply that it gives information beforehand which is verified by the event?

The meaning of Fulfilment goes much deeper than this. St. Paul says in Gal. 5. 14 and more fully in Rom. 13. 8–10 that 'love is the fulfilment of the Law'. He says in the latter passage that the Commandments (VI–IX) about man's duty to his neighbour are summed up in the words of Leviticus 19. 18, 'Thou shalt love thy neighbour as thyself'; so, if a man loves his neighbour with the love with which every man naturally loves himself, the Law is thereby fulfilled. But love cannot be tied to a meticulous observance of precepts; love proceeds from the heart, and deals with each particular situation as it arises in ways for which no precise rules can be given beforehand. The Law was drawn up in order to regulate man's observance of his duty to God and to his fellow-man. But Love goes straight to the end for which Law existed, and achieves it. So the Law is 'fulfilled' when it ceases to be mere law and becomes love. In being 'fulfilled', the Law is transformed.

It is in this sense that our Lord comes 'not to destroy but to fulfil' the Law and the Prophets (Matt. 5. 17). And this being so, it becomes certain that St. John's real purpose in quoting the fulfilment of Ps. 22. 18 is not merely to call attention to the fulfilment in detail, but much more to refer the reader back to Ps. 22 for the light which it throws on the mystery of victory through suffering, just as he refers to the Passover Lamb in verse 36, and to Zechariah 12. 10 and 13. 2 in verse 37, of John 19.

Since this is a book about the Old Testament and not the New, it will be possible to sketch out the outlines of the Fulfilment only in the briefest way, omitting all discussion of the problems of New Testament study. We must begin with the Hope of the Davidic Kingdom, whose origin was dealt with in chapter V (pp. 55–58); the Hope that was damped down when the Monarchy came to an end, but which flared up momentarily in Zerubbabel, 520–16 B.C. and vigorously in the first century B.C. What attitude did our LORD take to it?

THE MESSIAH, THE SON OF DAVID

The programme of his preaching is announced in Mark 1. 15:

> 'The time is fulfilled,
> And the Kingdom of God is at hand;
> Repent ye, and believe the Gospel.'

The fulfilment of the Hope of Israel is at hand, is 'upon you', is ready to break through; and the word Kingdom could suggest the promised Davidic Kingdom. Yet nowhere in any recorded saying of our Lord is there anything which speaks of the nationalistic idea of a political Kingdom, and much which contradicts it, such as Matt. 8. 11–12 with the partial parallel in Luke 13. 28–30, or the parable of the Wicked Husbandmen in Mark 12. 1–9; and in the account of his Temptation in the Wilderness, Matt. 4. 8–10, Luke 4. 5–8, he explicitly rejects the offer of 'all the kingdoms of the world and the glory of them'.

He shows a marked reserve with regard to the titles of 'Messiah' (Christ) and Son of David. The title of 'Christ' is of course freely used in the Acts and the Epistles; but these belong to the period after his crucifixion and resurrection, when the cross had made the idea of a political Kingdom completely impossible. During the Ministry, he does not use the title 'Christ' of himself; he accepts it when others use it of him, but substitutes for it the title 'Son of man' (see Mark 8. 29 and 31; 14. 61–62), and it is this title which comes again and again in the predictions of his passion (Mark 8. 31; 9. 12, 31; 10. 33, 45; 14. 21, 44). Similarly he accepts the title 'Son of David' from blind Bartimaeus, Mark 10. 47–48 (cf. also Matt. 9. 27–29 and 15. 22).

He is transforming the Messianic Hope in fulfilling it. His reply to the Tempter's offer of temporal power is given in the words of Deut. 6. 13, 'Thou shalt worship the LORD thy God, and him only shalt thou serve'; for indeed a political Kingdom, in all its glory and success, would not be the Reign or Kingly Rule of God, but a caricature of it and a substitute for it. It would not be the Kingdom of God, but one of the kingdoms of the world.

What way, then, did he follow instead? What did he actually do and say? It was not that he gave up the seeking of a Kingdom, or ceased to think of himself as King; it was that the Kingdom was God's Kingdom, and the word and the idea needed to be re-interpreted in a different sense, and implemented in a different way. The thing which was to happen was that the LORD God should reign over men, reign over their hearts and minds and wills, and men return to an attitude of entire obedience to him. This would be a very different thing from an earthly kingdom in which the Messiah held the temporal power.

Once two disciples came to him seeking to be promised the chief places in his Kingdom. He replied that they did not know what they were asking for; were they prepared to drink of his cup and be baptized with his baptism? (Mark 10. 35–38). He followed this up with some words to all the Twelve about the nature of authority: The rulers of the nations use their authority as an opportunity to domineer over men; but that is a false notion of their calling, contrary to the truth. In his Kingdom the true principle is to be acted upon: namely that the ruler is the general servant of all, called to bear the burdens of all. Of this the pattern is the Son of Man, who came not to be ministered unto but to minister, and to give his life a ransom for many (Mark 10. 42–45).

On his disciples he made an unqualified demand for loyalty and obedience to him; yet that demand rested simply on obedience to the truth. To them he was no despot, fascinating them with his personality and robbing them of their freedom: for in being his disciples they became free and became truly themselves:

'If ye abide in my word, then are ye truly my disciples: and ye shall know the Truth: and the Truth shall make you free' (John 8. 31–32).

But this was possible for them only on the basis of the most radical self-criticism. For the Lord insisted on digging right down in the human soul till he came to rock-bottom; and this meant the exposure of all vanity, self-deceit and wishful thinking, particularly of the religious variety. Seen in this very searching light, the Pharisees, who were the religious people of the day, appeared as 'hypocrites': it was not that they were conscious frauds, but that inwardly and in their secret hearts they were not godly men. 'I know you, that ye have not the love of God in yourselves' (John 5. 42). On the other hand, many 'sinners' (women of loose lives; men who were outcast from decent society through working as 'publicans', or tax-collectors), when they were faced with the same exposure of the secrets of their hearts, accepted it and found forgiveness and peace.

So he went among men, proclaiming the Kingly Rule of God, and meaning what he said. He had come, as he put it, longing to gather together the people of Israel 'as a hen gathereth her chickens under her wing' (Matt. 23. 27), that Israel might be truly the People of God, under the leadership of him whom the Father had sent. It was the fulfilment of all that to which the Old Testament had been moving, the consummation of its whole spiritual development, the accomplishment of the Purpose of God for his chosen people. The LORD whose way had so long been prepared, had come, as the prophet had said: 'The LORD, whom ye seek, shall suddenly come to his Temple' (Mal. 3. 1, continuation of the quotation in Mark 1. 2).

To the Temple Jesus came. His entry into the city on Palm Sunday appears to have been planned by him to correspond with the terms of a famous prophecy which spoke of Jerusalem's King coming to her, lowly and riding on an ass, and declared that this king would cut off the battle-bow and the war-horse, and would speak peace to the nations, and exercise universal rule (see Zech. 9.

9–10). Had he regarded himself as destined for temporal power, he would have been on a war-horse. Next day he entered the Temple, and expelled the traders who held a market there, changing foreign into Jewish money and selling animals for sacrifice. It was not merely that he saw an evil thing going on and intervened to stop it; it was that he had come to his Temple, where he as God's chosen had authority. That this is so is proved by the immediate reaction on the part of the Chief Priests; they asked him outright 'By what authority doest thou these things?'

By entering Jerusalem in state and by assuming authority in the Temple, he had posed the Chief Priests, and the people generally, with a question which demanded an answer. Would they acknowledge him as the promised King of Israel? Or would they destroy him? It must be one or the other. No evasion was possible.

They had him crucified, by sentence of Pontius Pilate, in order that he might die the death to which a particular curse was attached —'he that is hanged [on a tree] is accursed of God', from Deut. 21. 23—so that every Jew who heard of it would say that this Jesus was an impious pretender to the highest of all functions, on whom God had broken out, causing him to be denounced by his High-Priest and condemned to that accursed death. But his disciples, who on that Good Friday night were completely broken men (for the meaning of the curse attached to the cross could not escape them), tell us of the tomb being found empty on the third day, and how they saw him risen, and how within seven weeks they were proclaiming, in the very city where he had been crucified, that God had raised him from the dead, reversing the sentence which men had pronounced.

The Gospel was true: this was the promised King. God had established his kingdom, in spite of the resistance of rebellious men. God's love had proved stronger than human hate. No power of earth or of hell could prevent the 'Stone which the builders rejected' going into its place as the corner-stone (Mark 12. 10).

In St. John's Gospel it is made plain how the Crucified is the true King. In John 18. 36 it is explained that his kingdom is not of (from) this world: if it were, he would have an army and a police to protect him: and in verse 37 that he is the universal spiritual King, who is come to 'bear witness unto the truth'—the truth about God, and about men, and about every man, you and me. In 19. 14 Pilate shows him to the Jews: 'Behold, your King'; and they, in order to disown him, are compelled to say that they have no King but Caesar. Nothing remains then but that Jesus should be crucified; and he is crucified with the title over his head 'Jesus of Nazareth, the King of the Jews', written in the three languages which mattered in the ancient world (verses 19–20). If Jesus had claimed temporal power, his Crucifixion would be the final disproof of that claim. But if his Kingship was what he said it was and what he proved it to be in his relations with his disciples, his royal claim and his kingly character are in no way affected by what his enemies did to him; rather, he when he is lifted up from the earth, draws all men to himself (John 12. 32).

Such is our Lord's Kingship, and such his authority. Here we see how the Christian Church becomes different from Old Israel. Old Israel was called to bear witness to God's spiritual claim; but this spiritual authority was confused with the temporal authority of its civil rulers, when it was an independent state. The Christian Church exists in all nations side by side with the civil power; but it can never rightly hold the temporal power, since it becomes false to its own nature whenever it tries to do so. Its regular teaching is that the civil ruler rules by God's ordinance. Men must 'render unto Caesar the things that are Caesar's, and to God the things that are God's' (Mark 12. 17)—in other words, there is a duty owed to Caesar, but not an absolute duty, for there are things that are not Caesar's. This is the principle that the State transgresses when it becomes totalitarian, and claims control over men's minds and consciences: for man's mind and conscience are created to respond to God's truth, and of that truth the Church is sent to bear witness, in Christ's name (John 18. 37). Church and State have their respective functions, and each needs the other.

We come next to the prophecies with which we dealt in chapter VIII, relating to the new Exodus and Covenant, the Spirit, the

Return of the Presence, the Calling in of the Gentiles; but it will be convenient to alter the order, because we have said little hitherto of the great Controversy with the Pharisees which led up to his crucifixion, and the prophecies throw light on this. Why did they bring him to the death of the cross? For no one would trouble to crucify a Teacher who told attractive parables about men's moral duty. It was a controversy of the most radical kind.

THE GIFT OF THE SPIRIT

We have dealt with the prophecies of this Messianic Gift on pp. 88–89. But the perplexing question of what the Holy Spirit is receives unexpected light from a perplexing passage in the gospels, Mark 4. 11–12. Here our Lord quotes Isaiah 6. 9–10, where the prophet, after his vision of the Glory of the LORD in the Temple, is made aware that those to whom he must go will prove to be men of unseeing eyes and ears that are no better than deaf, because they will not listen nor understand. And with our Lord's mission it is the same: that

> 'Seeing they may see, and not perceive,
> And hearing they may hear, and not understand,
> Lest haply they should turn again,
>   And it should be forgiven them' (Mark 4. 12).

It is the word 'lest' that is perplexing; for the teaching was most certainly designed, not to prevent people from seeing the truth, but to reveal it to them. But there *was* something that prevented them, and it was something within themselves; if that internal hindrance were broken down, they would at once turn again and be healed and forgiven. Such must be the meaning of the word 'lest'; and it was not simply a question of the Parables and their interpretation, but rather of his whole message and mission. (So Dr. Jeremias explains in his great book on *The Parables of Jesus*, pp. 14 ff.)

How else was it possible for the Scribes, as has been told in the previous chapter of St. Mark, 3. 22–30, to look on him casting out devils (restoring epileptics to health and lunatics to sanity) and say that he was in league with the Evil One? Our Lord treated this accusation most seriously, as a sign of deadly sin (28–30). For in truth his ministry of healing of body and souls was a sign that God's Kingdom was at hand, was present, was breaking in:

'If I by the finger of God cast out devils, then is the Kingdom of God come upon you' (Luke 11. 20).

And his words in Matt. 11. 5.

> 'The blind receive their sight,
> The lame walk,
> The lepers are cleansed,
> And the deaf hear,
> And the dead are raised up,
> And the poor have Good Tidings preached to them',

were very recognizable as an echo of the description in Isaiah 35. 5–6 of the things that would happen when the LORD's Day of Salvation came:

> 'Then shall the eyes of the blind be opened,
> And the ears of the deaf shall be unstopped;
> Then shall the lame man leap as a hart,
> And the tongue of the dumb shall sing.'

In truth he had come to heal the whole man, in body and soul, for again and again we find bodily healing coupled with the forgiveness of sins (e.g. Mark 2. 1–12), the healing of the paralytic; and compare Mark 5. 34 with Luke 7. 50. Yet men were blind to it; these things were hidden from the 'wise and prudent' (Matt. 11. 25–26).

Is not this power to see what is plainly true, when you *see* it, when the internal hindrances of 'blindness' and 'deafness' are broken down, just what is meant by the work of the Holy Spirit, to whom we pray

> 'Enable with perpetual light,
> The dullness of our blinded sight'?

In the gospels, the Spirit is seen descending on our Lord at his baptism, as on the Messianic King (Isa. 11. 2–3, p. 58 above); and after his work of redemption is complete, the Spirit descends upon men at Pentecost, when St. Peter explains that this is the Messianic Gift, of which the prophet Joel had spoken (Acts 2. 16–21).

There is much more to be said about the Holy Spirit, but this is the starting-point. When in John 16. 13 our Lord says that the Spirit 'shall guide you into all truth', this does not mean that the apostles and their successors in the Church will be infallible, but that the Spirit will be at hand to show to them the plain and simple things, to break up their self-conceit and teach them humility, and to show them how in ministering to other people they are really ministering to their Lord.

THE NEW COVENANT

We have seen how the New Covenant and the Gift of the Spirit are closely related (pp. 88–89 above); for the great prophecy in Jer. 31. 31–34 speaks of a fourfold gift (i) God's Law written in men's hearts, so that (ii) they will be truly his people, (iii) knowing him at first-hand, and (iv) receiving forgiveness of sin.

In 2 Cor. 3 St. Paul is clearly thinking of this when he writes:

'You yourselves are our Letter of Recommendation, written on your hearts, to be known and read by all men; and you show that you are a Letter from Christ, delivered by us, written not with ink but with the Spirit of the living God, not on tablets of stone but on tablets of human hearts.'

Then he says that our sufficiency as apostles

'is from God, who has qualified us to be ministers of a New Covenant, not in a written code but in the Spirit; for the written code kills, but the Spirit gives life' (2 Cor. 3. 2–3, 5–6, R.S.V.).

These words of St. Paul take us straight back to the gospels, for he is teaching just what our Lord had taught in his controversy with the Pharisees. A central point in the controversy had been our Lord's dealings with the 'publicans' (tax-collectors under the Roman Government, such as Zacchaeus, Luke 19. 1–10) and 'sinners' (who might be fallen women, such as the penitent who came to him in Luke 7. 36–50). The complaint against him was,

' "He eateth and drinketh with publicans and sinners." And when Jesus heard it, he saith unto them, "They that are whole have no need of a physician, but they that are sick: I came not to call the righteous, but sinners".' (Mark 2. 16–17.)

They complained that he kept bad company: people like that needed to be reproved and told to amend their lives, to give up their sins and attend the synagogue every Sabbath and keep the Law. They themselves were tempted, like us 'respectable' Christians today, to compare ourselves with others who do not live up to our standard, and regard ourselves as those whose merits entitle them to receive God's reward. God punishes sinners, and rewards the godly; righteous people produce the fruits of Good Works, and these deserve respect and recognition from God and men.

Our LORD exposed this kind of thing quite mercilessly in the Parable of the Pharisee and the Publican (Luke 18. 9-14), in which the Pharisee is shown to have no real need for God at all; for all that he does in his prayer is to remind God of his own virtues, while the other, who is a sinner and knows it, pleads for God's mercy and receives it.

Our LORD went among the 'sinners' as those who needed the Physician, who made no claim of merit for themselves, and knew that they needed help. Can we imagine how he went among them? Surely he went among them not to stand as it were on a pedestal and preach down to them, but quite the opposite: to be interested in them as persons, to want to know about their homes and their interests, to let them talk to him. They for their part had never met a 'godly man' like this before; and many of them responded with much love, like the penitent woman in Luke 7, whose sins which were many were forgiven, because she loved much.

Luke 15 has three parables about the 'publicans and sinners', the Lost Sheep, the Lost Coin, and the Lost Son. The first two end on the note of the joy in heaven over the sinner who repents; and as for the third, we can imagine our Lord asking a question of his hearers at the end, as he often did: 'Which of the two, do you think, acted rightly to the returning wastrel—the father who welcomed him home, or the elder brother who would not speak to him?'

Our Lord here issued a challenge to the whole mentality of the godly Pharisee, to whom the strict observance of the Law was everything, but who were further away from God than the 'sinners';

and it could be that this, almost more than anything else, made them determined to get rid of him. If only he would go into retirement in Galilee, it would not matter, and they would leave him alone. But he had come with the Gospel of the Kingdom of God, and he pressed the challenge home.

All are sinners; the ungodly people to whom our Lord went knew it, but the godly ones mostly did not. As St. Paul puts it,

'God hath shut up all unto disobedience, that he might have mercy upon all' (Romans 11. 32).

And this is what he means by 'Justification by Faith'. The Christian is made right with God, and is brought to be at peace with God, not in virtue of 'the works of the law', not through attaining any Pharisaic standard of religion and morals, not through any virtues or merits of his own, not through any religiousness of his own. He is brought to be at peace with God simply because Christ came as the Saviour of the world; and 'faith' means simply accepting this, and saying, 'I am a weak and sinful man, on whom God has laid his hand.'

So it is that when our Lord says at the institution of the Holy Eucharist, 'This chalice is the New Covenant in my Blood', the promised New Covenant is brought into existence through the sacrifice (blood) of the Messiah; and the Eucharist is the sacrament of his sacrifice. And that which has been effected once for all *for* us through the coming of the Saviour and his death and resurrection, must then be effected *in* us by the coming of the Holy Spirit.

THE SECOND EXODUS

The original Exodus had been a mighty act of the LORD, to deliver a mob of slaves into political freedom. The second Exodus to which the prophets looked forward was to be a mighty act of the LORD, a consummation of his purpose for Israel when he brought them back from exile; it was still to be a deliverance into political freedom, but it was to be the deliverance of a penitent and converted people. The Exodus which our Lord accomplished at Jerusalem (Luke 9. 31) by his death and resurrection was another mighty act of the LORD, not bringing any change of political conditions, but delivering a penitent people from the power of the real Enemy of mankind, from the Evil One, from the Sin which is the love of the self.

'Christ our Passover Lamb is sacrificed for us', says St. Paul, 'therefore let us keep the Festival, not with the leaven of malice and wickedness [like Caiaphas in the Passover which he kept that year], but with the unleavened bread of sincerity and truth' (1 Cor. 5. 7–8). The festival of which he speaks can well be that of Easter, which has always been and is today specially connected with the thought of the Second Exodus. And if we follow Dr. Jeremias in his book *The Eucharistic Words of Jesus* (pp. 144–6), the identification of Jesus with the true Passover Lamb may well have been made by himself at the Last Supper; for if the Last Supper was the Passover-meal, the lamb of the Jewish rite will have been on the table, and when he said 'This is my body' amidst the sacrificial associations of the occasion it would be plain that the Sacrifice of the New Covenant stood in contrast with that of the Old.

The Second Exodus was his passion and resurrection. St. Paul develops this thought in 1 Cor. 10. 1–4, which we may paraphrase thus: 'Our forefathers at the Exodus were overshadowed by the divine Presence in the Pillar of Cloud, and went through a sort of "baptism by water" at the Crossing of the Red Sea, and later on in the wilderness they had the divinely given food of the Manna, and drank of the Water from the Rock. Just so you Christians of Corinth were in the divine Presence at your conversion and your baptism, and this was your Exodus; and now at the Lord's Supper you have the eucharistic bread and cup.' He continues, in verses 5–10: 'Beware therefore lest you fall into the sins into which our forefathers fell in their wilderness-wanderings: the lusts of the flesh, idolatry (cf. 1 Cor. 8. 10), fornication (cf. 6. 13–20), tempting the LORD (cf. 10. 19–22), murmuring (against your Apostle, as they murmured against Moses). That generation of Israelites lost their inheritance in their Promised Land; and so may you, in yours.'

(There is a fuller treatment of the Second Exodus, with some references to the Easter liturgy and hymns, in my book *When Israel came out of Egypt*, chapter V.)

THE RETURN OF THE PRESENCE

The Presence of the LORD which had been manifested in the Pillar of Cloud and had dwelt upon the sacred Ark, was to return to dwell in the rebuilt Temple (Ezek. 43. 1–7, p. 90 above); the House would be filled with his Glory (Hag. 2. 7); he would dwell in the midst of his people. Perhaps the author of Chronicles imagined it as like his account of the dedication of Solomon's Temple (p. 111 above).

But St. John speaks of the Return of the Presence quite otherwise:

> 'The Word was made flesh,
> And dwelt among us,
> (And we beheld his Glory,
> Glory as of the only-begotten from the Father)
> Full of grace and truth.' (John 1. 14.)

The word 'dwelt' recalls in the directest way such a phrase as 'the place which the LORD thy God shall choose to cause his Name to *dwell* there'; for St. John's Greek word *eskenose* reproduces the consonants of the Hebrew *shakhan*, to dwell, *mishkhan*, the Tabernacle, *Shekhinah*, the Presence. The word 'Glory' had been repeatedly used of the Presence, as we have seen, pp. 90–91. In St. John the word is used here, in 1. 14, of the sacred humanity of our Lord; in 2. 11 he manifests his Glory in his 'beginning of miracles' at Cana, which was as it were a bright point where the Glory shone out, so that his disciples believed on him; and from 12. 23 onwards, the words 'glory' and 'glorify' are used repeatedly of his passion, as being the supreme manifestation of the divine love.

Thus the Presence never returned to the sanctuary of that Temple whose outer court our Lord cleansed; that Temple made with hands was destroyed by Titus in A.D. 70. St. John, quoting a saying which according to Mark 14. 56–59 was quoted against our Lord at his trial in a garbled form, gives as its true form 'Destroy this temple and in three days I will raise it up' (John 2. 19), and adds the comment, 'But he spake of the temple of his body' (verse 21). The place where the Presence dwelt was first the humanity of Jesus; his body was raised from the dead after three days. It is also the

Church which is his body: for it is this that is now the real Temple of God—the people, not the church-building constructed of bricks and timber. The people are the Church. The people are the living stones of the Temple (1 Pet. 2. 5).

This teaching runs through the New Testament. Our Lord implied it when he spoke of himself as the stone which the builders rejected, but which would become the head corner-stone (Mark 12. 10, quoting Ps. 118. 22–23). St. Paul is explicit: the Corinthian Christians are a Temple of God, and the Spirit of God dwells in them (1 Cor. 3. 16, 17); they are the Sanctuary in which the Presence dwells. In 2 Cor. 6. 16 he quotes, with a difference, a text from Lev. 26. 11, 12, in which God says that he will set his Tabernacle (*mishkhan*) *among* his People and walk among them: St. Paul has it, 'For we are a temple of the living God: even as God said, I will dwell *in* them, and walk in them.' In 1 Cor. 6. 19 each Christian's body is called a temple, because the Holy Ghost dwells there. But properly it is the community that is the temple. In Eph. 2. 20–22 it is the whole Church universal, composed of Jews and Gentiles; built on the foundation of the apostles and prophets, Christ Jesus being the great corner-stone which underlies them; built up, by the building into it of all the members. In the vision of 'heaven' in Revelation, there is no visible temple; 'for the LORD God Almighty and the Lamb are the temple thereof' (21. 22). Once again, then, the prophecy is transformed in being fulfilled.

There is a similar transformation in the idea of the sacrifices which were offered in the Temple. Under the old law a worshipper brought an animal or other prescribed offering; though prophets and psalmists told him that what God really wanted was that he should give himself to God to do his will. One psalmist understood that this was the real sacrifice, the reality of which the animal sacrifices were only a symbol:

'Thou desirest no sacrifice, else would I give it thee;
Thou delightest not in burnt offerings:
The sacrifice of God is a troubled spirit;
A broken and a contrite heart, O God, thou wilt not despise'
   (Ps. 51. 16–17).

Second Isaiah saw that the martyrdom of the Suffering Servant had been ordained by God as a sacrifice for sin, acceptable to himself (Isa. 53.10).

So it was that our Lord, at the Last Supper, by using sacrificial words over the bread and wine, interpreted his death as the supreme Sacrifice: and so it is that in the Eucharist the Church recalls and re-enacts this Sacrifice, and in it the communicants in being united to the Lord are themselves offered up in sacrifice, with him and in him.

As then the Temple of the Old Covenant finds its fulfilment in a temple built of human souls, and in these the Presence dwells; so the animal-sacrifices offered by men are fulfilled in the One Sacrifice of God's own Passover Lamb, and the worshippers cannot celebrate his Sacrifice without themselves being offered up in him. There is a real continuity of idea. It is not that the idea found in the Old Testament is discarded, and something different substituted for it; our Lord is come not to destroy, but to fulfil, the Law and the Prophets (Matt. 5. 17); in him we see that towards which the Old Testament is moving.

Therefore when we use the Old Testament, we do not have to discard phrases like Jerusalem, Zion, the sanctuary, or the priest's preparation for sacrifice (as in Ps. 26) or the description of the rite of the burnt-offering. We should have to discard them if they referred only to an order of things which had passed away. But we can use them if we know, as every Christian ought to know, how they are fulfilled in Christ and have become woven into the texture of Christian devotion. Thus, if we may dare to paraphrase Heb. 9. 11–14:

'Christ is the High Priest of the Messianic order: He offers his sacrifice in no temple made with hands, situated in this created world, but in the Heavenly Temple; and his Sacrifice is no oblation of the blood of goats and calves, but is his own blood; and he has entered in once for all into that Sanctuary, having won an eternal, not merely a temporal, deliverance. The effect of his Sacrifice is not such a cleansing from outward and ceremonial defilement as was effected by sprinkling the blood of bulls or goats or a heifer, but the cleansing and sanctifying of human hearts and minds to render to the living God that service which they owe him, through the pure and sinless self-oblation of the Saviour in the power of the eternal Holy Spirit.'

THE COMING IN OF THE GENTILES

We have seen how Israel knew that it had the duty laid upon it of bringing the knowledge of the true God to the Gentiles, but was unable to fulfil it. Approaches were indeed made to the Gentile world in the Wisdom literature, and the synagogues all over the eastern Mediterranean world exercised a powerful attraction, both by their liturgy and the teaching given there. But the fact remained that the Greek could not become a member of the believing and worshipping community without leaving his own nation and becoming a Jew. Consequently there were thousands of people, called in the New Testament 'worshippers' (Acts 16. 14) or 'God-fearers' (Acts 13. 16), who remained sitting as it were on the doorstep of the synagogue, but refusing to be circumcised and become 'proselytes' (Acts 13. 43).

Our LORD's own mission was to Israel, to 'gather her children together like a hen gathering her chickens under her wing' (Matt. 23. 27), that she might truly be the People of the LORD, under its Messiah; *then* it would fulfil its duty to the Gentile world. To the superficial observer, it would seem that his mission failed. Actually, his mission did not fail; it succeeded, it was carried through, at the cost of his life; and consequently we find, within a few years of his death, the mission to the Gentiles going forward.

Here we come across one peculiarly interesting instance of 'fulfilment'. We noticed earlier (p. 93) that the prophets speak of the coming-in of the Gentiles as a movement towards a centre—Jerusalem. Now, in the fulfilment, this is what is seen to be happening. It is true that missionaries go out and make long journeys; but they go to call the people of many nations into a unity, which can indeed be called 'Zion' or 'Jerusalem' (in the transformed sense), but actually is Jesus Christ. So we find, in the vision of the Church on earth in Rev. 14. 1–3:

K

'And I saw, and behold the Lamb standing on the mount Zion, and with Him a hundred and forty and four thousand, having His Name and the Name of His Father, written on their foreheads.'

Then St. John becomes aware of the heavenly worship which he has described in chapters 4 and 5, and that the echo of that worship is audible to the Church on earth; for

'No man could learn that song save the hundred and forty and four thousand, who had been redeemed from the earth' (verse 3).

Christ is the Centre of Unity for mankind; for 'He is our peace, who hath made both [Jew and Gentile] one, and hath broken down the middle wall of partition [the boundary wall surrounding the inner sanctuary of the Temple at Jerusalem, past which no Gentile might go, under pain of death] . . . for through him we both [Jew and Gentile] have access by one Spirit to the Father' (Eph. 2. 14, 18).

This began to happen quite soon after our LORD's resurrection. According to the Acts of the Apostles, the signal for it was given by St. Stephen's martyrdom, which was followed by a series of initiatives:

Philip goes to Samaria (detested though it was by the Jews), and preaches the Gospel there (8. 5–13); and his mission there is endorsed by the Apostles Peter and John (8. 14–25).

Philip baptizes an Ethiopian eunuch, a 'worshipper' (8. 27); but this has no sequel in the Acts (8. 26–40).

The persecutor of the Christians, Saul the Pharisee, is converted, to become the Apostle of the Gentiles (9. 1–30).

Peter is called upon to go to Joppa, by a Roman centurion who is a 'God-fearer' (10. 1); as a Jew, he has scruples about eating with Gentiles, but these are taken away by a vision which confirms a lesson learnt from the Master long before (Mark 7. 15). So he preaches the Gospel there, and these Gentile converts are baptized. When he next visits Jerusalem, some of the Christians there likewise have scruples; but he tells his story, which shows that the Messianic Gift of the Spirit has been given to these Gentiles, as to themselves at Pentecost. It is the hand of the LORD, and there is no more to be said (11. 15–18).

Next, some who had been scattered by the persecution that followed Stephen's martyrdom went far afield to Phoenicia, Cyprus and Antioch; and here some of them began to preach the Gospel 'to Greeks also' (11. 20). So the Church at Antioch became a mixed community of Jews and Greeks, and it was from Antioch that St. Paul's mission journeys started, in Acts 13.

We, too, are Gentile Christians; and if we have our problems with regard to the interpretation and use of the Old Testament, we see that the first generation of Christians had their difficulties too. Perhaps very much of the problem arises from our Lord's own task with the Old Testament, not to destroy but to fulfil, to make complete, and so in a measure to transform, the word spoken in the Law and by the Prophets.

We see how it was in the first generation. The Council of Jerusalem opened the door to the Gentile mission, by laying on the Gentile converts nothing beyond four necessary things which would make it possible for Jews and Gentiles to live together in one Church (Acts 15. 28–29).

It was to be the Gospel and not the Law. Salvation, Justification and the Forgiveness of sins came not as the reward of meritorious Law-keeping, but purely as God's own gift through the Messiah Jesus, received with the faith which was self-committal. The Jewish Christians were free to keep the Law as they always had done. But the Gentile Christians were not to be circumcised, nor keep the food-rules forbidding 'unclean' foods such as pork, nor were they bound by the rules of the Sabbath. Yet even these were not 'destroyed' but 'fulfilled'. Already in the Old Testament Deuteronomy had spoken a circumcision of the heart 'to love the LORD thy God with all thine heart and with all thy soul, that thou mayest live' (Deut. 30. 6); and so St. Paul could speak of the true circumcision as that 'of the heart, in the Spirit and not in the letter' [of the Law] (Rom. 2. 29). Similarly in the Collect for the Circumcision of our Lord (Jan. 1) we pray for 'the true circumcision of the Spirit, that our hearts and all our members being mortified from all worldly and carnal lusts, we may in all things obey thy blessed will'.

So it is with the Law of Uncleanness. Ps. 51. 2 prays 'Wash me thoroughly from my wickedness, and cleanse me from my sin'; and so our Lord had taught that a man is not made 'unclean' by the food that goes into his mouth, but by the bad words that come out of it (Mark 7. 15); and St. Paul applies the principle in Rom. 14. 14, 'I know and am persuaded in the Lord Jesus [i.e. in his recorded teaching] that nothing is unclean of itself', and 'the Kingdom of God is not eating and drinking, but righteousness and peace and joy in the Holy Ghost' (verse 17).

The Sabbath is 'fulfilled', not primarily in the substitution of Sunday for Saturday, but rather in the fact that 'there remaineth therefore a Sabbath-rest for the People of God' (Heb. 4. 9); and an early Christian writer, Justin Martyr, says that 'the New Law desires you to keep Sabbath always'.

There were of course, and there still are, perils in such freedom, and it is clear that St. Paul's Corinthians fell into them, taking it that freedom means doing what you please. St. Paul found it necessary to give them rules to keep, as e.g. in 1 Cor. 10. 23–33, with regard to meat sold in the market, which might or might not have been killed for some pagan sacrifice. On the other side, the Jewish Christians of Jerusalem were very conscious of the need for spiritual discipline, as we see in the Epistle of St. James.

There were these practical problems in the apostolic age, just as today, with regard to the use of the Old Testament. Yet the Church always needs the Old Testament; and it meant everything to the Church that from the beginning it was founded on *Jewish monotheism*, that there is one God only, who has revealed himself in history; on a *Jewish Messianism* for which there could be no shadow of doubt that he whom the Father had sent into the world was true man; and on a *Jewish understanding of the Holy Spirit*, that he is the Spirit who spoke by the prophets.

CHAPTER XII

'The First and the Last'

THE ADVENT OF THE LORD

THIS book began with a study of the Creation-poem: 'In the Beginning, God . . .' Then we thought about the Fall of Man, and then followed out the Story of Salvation from the Call of Abraham to the Fulfilment in Jesus the Messiah. God is the Beginning and the End, the First and the Last.

The Fulfilment in Messiah Jesus was the End. Yet it has not been the End, for history still goes on, and we are in the midst of it, engaged in making it, and the story of the world and of the Church is still unfinished. What do we make of this? Dr. John Robinson, now Bishop of Woolwich, has given us a book entitled *In the End, God*; the point of this title is that it contains a question to be answered. What will God do in the End? What is the End of his purpose? We say in the Creed, 'And he shall come again with glory to judge both the quick and the dead: whose Kingdom shall have no end'; and the Bible ends with the words, 'Amen: come, Lord Jesus.'

THE BOOK OF JOB

We can get light on these things from the Book of Job. We said nothing of this book in our study of the Old Testament history, because it is impossible to place the narrative-prologue and epilogue anywhere in the history, and we cannot even say with any certainty in which century it was written, except that it appears to have been written after the Exile. It is commonly described as a treatise on the mystery of Suffering; but this is not correct, for its subject is rather the whole problem of man's life and the possibility of faith in God.

It is a dialogue between Job and his three friends, Eliphaz, Bildad and Zophar. Job is in great suffering, and the three friends all take the line that since God punishes the wicked and rewards the righteous, it follows that since Job is suffering he must have sinned; let him then examine his conscience, find what his sin is, and repent. The three friends are like the people in all ages who know the answer to every question—the people who can tell us exactly what will happen in the first five minutes after death, and know just how God has predestined men from the beginning to heaven or to hell. Job indignantly repudiates this dogmatism, saying all the things which we associate with the 'freethinker', and how hard it is to believe in God when we look at the world and the things which happen in it.

But the climax of the book comes when the LORD himself takes part in the dialogue; he speaks to Job out of the whirlwind, as he who made the world and to whom it belongs. When he speaks, it is like the Day of Judgement. We are shown in the most vivid way the difference between the Reality of God and all men's notions and opinions and doctrines about him; the questions which the men have asked are not answered, nor is any solution propounded to the problem of suffering. But the book has done for us something better than this; for it has placed man's perplexities and man's sufferings in their true context. Man is in God's world, and he is the First and the Last. The answer lies not in any human wisdom, but in the purpose of him who created man.

In the prologue (chapters 1 and 2) we are introduced to Job as a righteous man, honoured and respected by all, and his life is pleasing to God. But then 'Satan' speaks (or rather, 'the Satan', 'the Adversary', who in this book is not specially diabolical, but is more like the 'Candid Friend'); he suggests that Job's admitted virtues are perhaps made rather easy by the fortunate conditions of his life (1. 9–10). Then in a moment Job loses everything, his sons and daughters and his great wealth; and still his faith stands firm (1. 20–22). But the Candid Friend can still point out that he is personally untouched and enjoys good health. At once Job is afflicted with foul disease; his wife loses her faith, but Job is still patient (2. 9–10).

Then the dialogue begins; there are three cycles of speeches by the friends in turn, in answer to speeches by Job. The friends have their stock answer to the problem, as we have said: since God punishes wickedness, Job's sufferings are a proof that he has committed some grave sin. Much of what they say is excellent; Eliphaz speaks beautifully of the fear due to God in 4. 12–21, Bildad of the ancient tradition of faith in 8. 8–22, and Zophar of the transcendence of God in 11. 1–12. But all the time they are seeking *security* in their cut-and-dried theology; they know where they stand.

Job altogether repudiates their arguments (13. 1–12), and he has no such security; for while he has a fundamental faith in God, he is not able to see how it works out in the actual experience of life. Does man on earth get a square deal? he is frail and helpless (7. 11–21, 14. 7–17). It looks as if God is unjust (19. 1–12); the friends are all wrong, for God does allow the wicked to prosper (21. 1–26). He sometimes wishes he had never been born (chapter 3, 10. 18–22). Does the actual course of the world suggest that there is a good God in charge?

Thus men are heard talking about God, and how he rules, or appears not to rule, his world. Then in the dramatic climax he himself appears. He asks Job two questions:

> 'Where wast thou when I laid the foundations of the earth?
> Declare, if thou hast understanding' (38. 4).

'Where were you when I created my world? Answer me that one!' The second is:

> 'Wilt thou even disannul My judgement?
> Wilt thou condemn Me, that you mayest be justified? (40. 8).

'Who are you to discern my plan for my universe, and sit in judgement upon it? Are you able to tell me how I ought to govern it?'

Job says in his final reply:

> 'I had heard of thee by the hearing of the ear;
> But now mine eye seeth THEE,
> Therefore I abhor myself,
> And repent in dust and ashes' (42. 5–6).

Now the matter has been put on its right basis. We men have 'heard about him by the hearing of the ear', we have talked about

God, we have put up our arguments to prove (or disprove) his existence, we have written treatises to justify (or impugn) the ways of God to men, and to show (or fail to show) why there is suffering in the world.

But no answer is given in the book to the questions which we men debate. We are not allowed by the book to put our trust in any apologetic that we can devise, or in any other man-made security of our own. We are taught that our Security is in God alone. For his is the Kingdom and the Power and the Glory; we are his small creatures, his little children. He is the Judge of mankind, and we are subject to his Judgement.

THE DAY OF THE LORD

Such is the help which the Book of Job gives us to grasp what the final Judgement of Mankind means. This however is a theme which the Old Testament does not make fully explicit. It does indeed tell the story of the Flood as the universal Judgement of God upon man's sin, and the prophet Zephaniah speaks of this Judgement in 1. 2–3. But on the whole the Old Testament thinks of the LORD's Judgement on sinful Israel, and on the nations which cruelly oppress her; the prophets long for the LORD to 'rend the heavens and come down' (Isa. 64. 1), that he may fight his own battle against the powers of evil (Isa. 59. 15–17, 20–21). The general emphasis is on the Messianic Hope in the wide sense of the term.

It is in the New Testament that the expectation of the coming Kingdom of God and the final Judgement becomes fully explicit. Here we are given a complete picture, expressed in Old Testament language:

'But in those days, after that tribulation,
 The sun shall be darkened,
 And the moon shall not give her light (Isa. 13. 10),
 And the stars shall be falling from heaven,
 And the powers that are in the heavens shall be shaken (Isa. 34. 4),
 And then shall they see the Son of man coming in clouds with great power and glory (Dan. 7. 13).

And then shall He send forth His angels,
And gather together His elect from the four winds
From the uttermost part of the earth to the uttermost part of heaven'
(Mark 13. 24–27).

But it is to be noticed here that he says nothing about the time, for
'of that day and that hour knoweth no one, not even the angels in
heaven, neither the Son, but the Father' (Mark 13. 32); nor is anything further said in this passage about what will follow, the Judgement and the everlasting Kingdom. When the Son of man has come,
all is in his hands, and we do not need to know any more. Just
so, in the Book of Job, when the LORD appears, the questions that
men have been asking were not answered: it is for the same reason.

THE FIRST ADVENT

But we have still one question to answer, about the relation of the
fulfilment of the prophecies of our Lord to the final fulfilment; or
in other words, of the First Advent of our Lord to his final Advent.

The necessary line of answer to this question is to see the difference in *the conditions of* the First and the Final Advents: the one is
'in the flesh' and in human lowliness, the other is 'in glory'. In the
gospels, the title 'Son of man' is used in these two senses: *first*,
'The Son of man hath not where to lay his head' (Matt. 8. 20), 'The
Son of man is come not to be ministered unto but to minister'
(Mark 10. 45), 'The Son of man must suffer many things' (Mark
8. 31); and *second*, 'The Son of man shall come in the glory of his
Father with the holy angels' (Mark 8. 38). That being so, there can
be a complete fulfilment of the 'Messianic Hope' by him *in the flesh*,
under human conditions, as true man, *and at the Final Advent*,
under different conditions, which we men who live in the flesh
cannot imagine, except by means of picture-images such as a
Descent upon the clouds of heaven, the trumpet sounding, the
heavenly wedding-feast, the New Jerusalem.

But then, there is the difference between him and us. He came
in the flesh, he suffered and died; but in it all he victoriously accomplished his mission, and he rose from the dead and entered into his

'glory'. But he left behind him disciples who were still very imperfect, and after them a vast multitude of others—including ourselves. We are all baptized into his death (Rom. 6. 3–6) and risen with him (Col. 3. 1), as sharers in his victory, sharers in the new life 'in Christ'. We belong to those who 'have not seen and yet have believed' (John 20. 29); ours is the life of faith, here on earth, in the flesh. We expect in the Future to enter on a life 'in glory' in the world beyond this. And yet at the same time we are sinners still, beset with troubles and temptations, from the 'Old Adam' within us, and the worldly world around us. We know that we have got to face the Final Judgement, when the truth of all things will be revealed.

This thought brings us back to the Book of Job. In that Book, as we have seen, all the persons in the story are judged. First there is Job's wife, who at the beginning has judged herself, for she has been prepared to 'curse God and die' (2. 9). Job is 'justified by faith', made right in God's sight, not in virtue of his upright life, nor of words wisely and rightly spoken, but simply because he has believed God to be God, and has faced up to him. Indeed, as he himself confesses, his words have been rash and presumptuous (42. 3); he acknowledges this, and he repents, seeing himself as he truly is in God's sight, an ignorant and sinful creature in the presence of the almighty Creator, and subject to his judgement. So it is that he is 'justified'. But the Three Friends, who have attempted to plead God's cause for him, and have sought security in their own notions and in the apologetic which they have put up, are not 'justified' at all.

And now for our question, about the relation of our Lord's Advent in the flesh to his Final Advent 'in glory': Do the essential characteristics of the Final Advent of the Son of Man appear when he comes 'in the flesh'?

In the gospel-records, there are those who are much in the position of Job's friends; they are seeking Security in a strict observance of the Law, and they judge the Lord Jesus by their own standards: how can he be from God when he does not keep the Sabbath in the manner prescribed by their rules? To them it is clear that our Lord's refusal to give a plain answer to a plain question was most annoying; he would not say whether it was lawful to give tribute to Caesar, nor define exactly who one's neighbour was, but insisted on raising the matter to another level. Again and again we find him confronting the hearer with the direct will of God, with a call to discipleship, with a searching statement of what discipleship involved. And it was because those men dared not forsake the false Security in which they trusted that they brought him to the death of the cross. These people were all 'judged'.

His disciples are seen in the gospels learning to trust themselves wholly to God and to him whom God had sent. But even so, it was terrifying when he told them that the Son of man must suffer—and this was too much for Peter, Mark 8, 32–33—and when he went on to say that all who would come after him must deny the self, to the point of being led out to be crucified too (verse 34), and when he went on to speak of the Final Judgement, and to say that whoever was ashamed of him and his words in that adulterous and sinful generation, the Son of man would be ashamed of him when he came 'in glory' (verse 38). His disciples too were 'judged'.

We are driven, as it seems, to say this: That while the Advent in the flesh and the Advent in glory are very different in their external shape and form, in their inner essence and reality they are one and the same. The Messianic prophecies really were fulfilled in Jesus, even though the world did not then come to an end, and history still went on. And the picture given us in the Book of Job of the final confrontation of Man with God finds its true Fulfilment in the words and acts and the passion and resurrection of Jesus in the flesh. When he came in the flesh, he came both as Judge and as Saviour.

AN INDEX OF NAMES AND SUBJECTS

Asterisks (*) denote quotations from the books or authors referred to.

PRINTED IN GREAT BRITAIN AT THE BOWERING PRESS, PLYMOUTH